SIGHT WORD RAINBOW
WORKSHEETS

Your students will vastly improve their reading and writing skills with these simple worksheets! Whether for instruction, practice or review, your students will master the 100 most common sight words in English. The predictable format allows all students to be successful. The limited vocabulary is also perfect for second language learners.

These reproducible worksheets are a great way to make learning sight words fun and easy.

WHAT IS THE SIGHT WORD RAINBOW?

We took the 100 most common words in English and divided them into six groups based on the difficulty in spelling. The RED group contains one and two letter words. The ORANGE group contains two letter and CVC words. The YELLOW level has slightly more difficult three letter words. The GREEN level contains 3 and 4 letter words, some non-phonetic and others with the long vowel sounds. Levels BLUE and PURPLE are made up of the more difficult words.

This title includes a worksheet for each of the 100 sight words in the Sight Word Rainbow program. However, being basic sight words, these pages can be used in *any* program.

HOW TO USE THE WORKSHEETS

Each worksheet is set up the same way, so that once students have seen how they are done, they are able to complete them on their own! This is a great whole class lesson, small group activity, or independent center task! It is also a great review page for homework.

Introduce the sight word to the class. Point out any silent letters, vowels that have a different sound, etc. If possible, relate the new word to words already known. For example the word "way" has the same ending as "day." The word "call" has the word "all" inside it.

You may have your students color the word at the top with a single color, in a pattern, or using one color for all of the consonants and another color for the vowels. Students can use a pencil, pen, colored pencil or even markers to trace and write the words and sentences.

WORD FUN!

At the bottom of each page (except for "I" and "a") are paper letter tiles that the students can cut out and rearrange to spell the sight word. These can also be used to spell other words that use the same letters. For example, using the letters for the word "this" you can also spell "his" and "is".

These letter tiles can be saved and used over and over, or have the students glue them in order on the back of the page.

RAINBOW WORDS

RED	ORANGE	YELLOW	GREEN	BLUE	PURPLE
I	do	and	was	each	many
a	to	see	who	down	said
at	by	how	one	very	were
up	my	now	will	long	they
an	or	her	look	into	from
if	of	for	like	your	call
in	as	day	them	what	after
is	can	may	then	when	first
it	had	you	made	come	there
on	has	out	make	some	their
be	him	its	more	find	these
he	his	all	time	most	where
we	did	the	than	only	which
go	not	she	just	over	words
no	get	are	with	have	other
so	but	use	this	been	little
					know
					about
					would
					could

Name: _______________________

1. Color the word.

a

a   a   a

2. Trace the word.

a   a   a   a   a

3. Write the word 5 times.

4. Trace the sentence and read it aloud.

I see a pig.

5. Write the sentence by yourself.

6. Close your eyes and spell the word.

7. Color the picture.

Name: _______________________

1. Color the word.

about
about   about

2. Trace the word.

about   about   about   about

3. Write the word 4 times.

4. Trace the sentence and read it aloud.

What is this book about?

5. Write the sentence by yourself.

6. Close your eyes and spell the word.
7. Color the picture.
8. Cut out the letters below, mix them up, and spell the word.

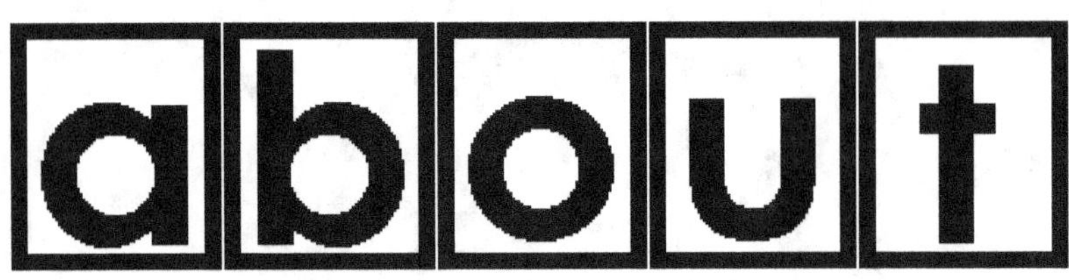

Name: ______________________

1. Color the word.

after

after   after

2. Trace the word.

after   after   after   after

3. Write the word 4 times.

4. Trace the sentence and read it aloud.

You may play after lunch.

5. Write the sentence by yourself.

©2020 SightWordRainbow.com

6. Close your eyes and spell the word.

7. Color the picture.

8. Cut out the letters below, mix them up, and spell the word.

Name: ______________________________

1. Color the word.

all

all all all all

2. Trace the word.

all all all all all

3. Write the word 5 times.

4. Trace the sentence and read it aloud.

I have all of them.

5. Write the sentence by yourself.

6. Close your eyes and spell the word.

7. Color the picture.

8. Cut out the letters below, mix them up, and spell the word.

a l l

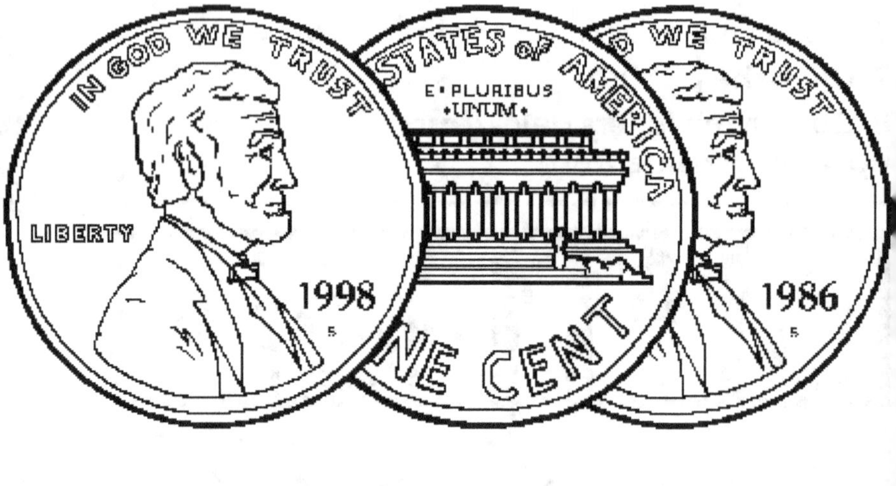

Name: ___________________________________

1. Color the word.

an

an   an   an   an

2. Trace the word.

an   an   an   an   an

3. Write the word 5 times.

4. Trace the sentence and read it aloud.

I see an apple.

5. Write the sentence by yourself.

6. Close your eyes and spell the word.
7. Color the picture.
8. Cut out the letters below, mix them up, and spell the word.

a n

1. Color the word.

and
and   and   and

2. Trace the word.

and   and   and   and   and

3. Write the word 5 times.

4. Trace the sentence and read it aloud.

I see a can and a man.

5. Write the sentence by yourself.

©2020 SightWordRainbow.com

6. Close your eyes and spell the word.
7. Color the picture.
8. Cut out the letters below, mix them up, and spell the word.

1. Color the word.

2. Trace the word.

3. Write the word 5 times.

4. Trace the sentence and read it aloud.

5. Write the sentence by yourself.

©2020 SightWordRainbow.com

6. Close your eyes and spell the word.
7. Color the picture.
8. Cut out the letters below, mix them up, and spell the word.

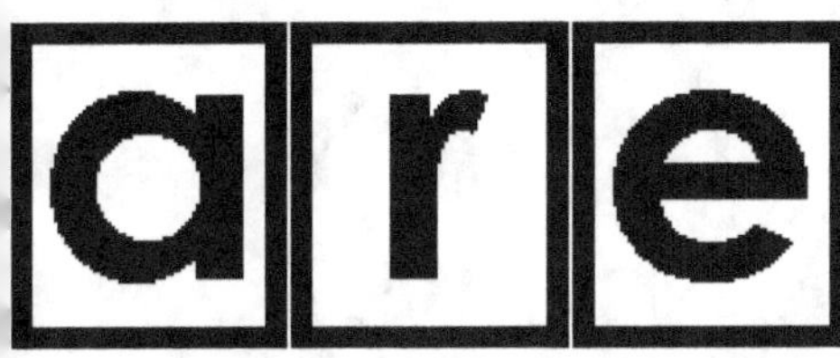

Name: ___________________________

1. Color the word.

as

as   as   as   as

2. Trace the word.

as   as   as   as   as

3. Write the word 5 times.

4. Trace the sentence and read it aloud.

I am as big as you.

5. Write the sentence by yourself.

6. Close your eyes and spell the word.
7. Color the picture.
8. Cut out the letters below, mix them up, and spell the word.

a s

Name: _______________________

1. Color the word.

at

at at at at

2. Trace the word.

at   at   at   at   at

3. Write the word 5 times.

4. Trace the sentence and read it aloud.

Do not look at the sun.

5. Write the sentence by yourself.

6. Close your eyes and spell the word.
7. Color the picture.
8. Cut out the letters below, mix them up, and spell the word.

a t

Name: _______________________________

1. Color the word.

be

be   be   be   be

2. Trace the word.

be   be   be   be   be

3. Write the word 5 times.

4. Trace the sentence and read it aloud.

I can be a cat.

5. Write the sentence by yourself.

©2020 SightWordRainbow.com

6. Close your eyes and spell the word.
7. Color the picture.
8. Cut out the letters below, mix them up, and spell the word.

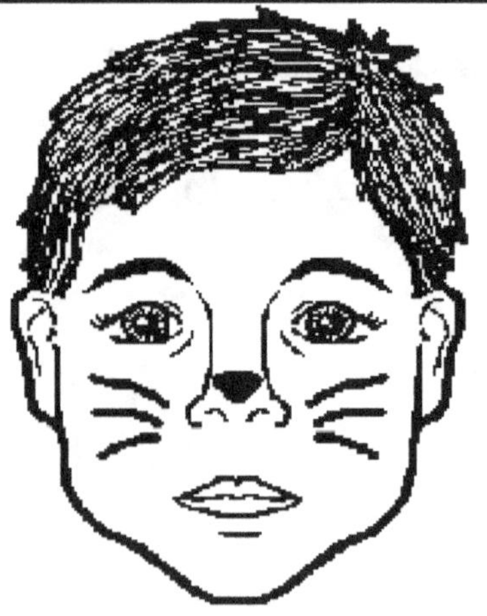

Name: ________________

1. Color the word.

been
been been been

2. Trace the word.

been   been   been   been

3. Write the word 4 times.

4. Trace the sentence and read it aloud.

I have been to the zoo.

5. Write the sentence by yourself.

©2020 SightWordRainbow.com

6. Close your eyes and spell the word.
7. Color the picture.
8. Cut out the letters below, mix them up, and spell the word.

b e e n

ZOO

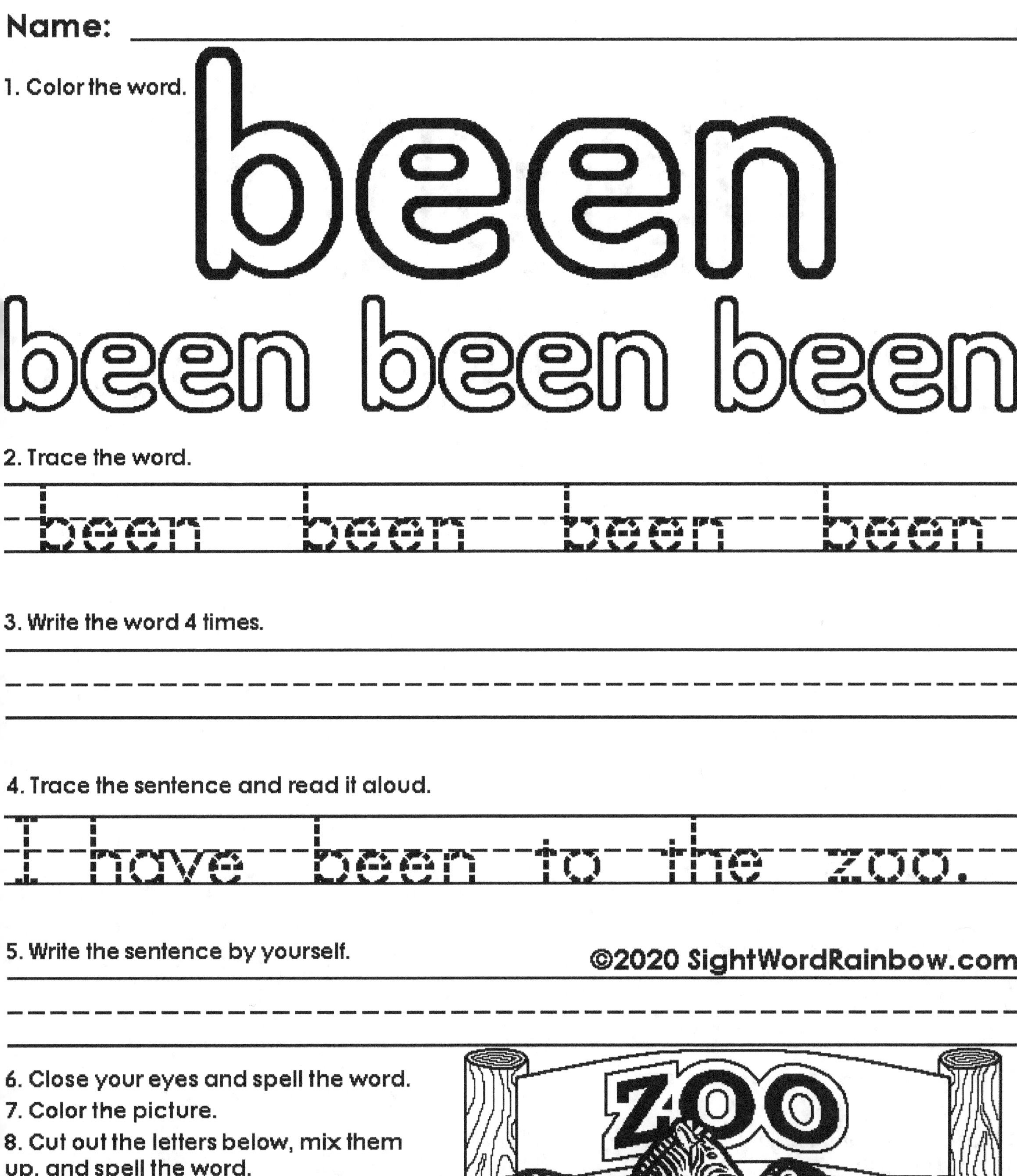

Name: ______________________________

1. Color the word.

2. Trace the word.

3. Write the word 5 times.

4. Trace the sentence and read it aloud.

5. Write the sentence by yourself.

©2020 SightWordRainbow.com

6. Close your eyes and spell the word.
7. Color the picture.
8. Cut out the letters below, mix them up, and spell the word.

Name: _______________________________

1. Color the word.

by

by   by   by

2. Trace the word.

by   by   by   by   by

3. Write the word 5 times.

4. Trace the sentence and read it aloud.

He is by the house.

5. Write the sentence by yourself.

6. Close your eyes and spell the word.
7. Color the picture.
8. Cut out the letters below, mix them up, and spell the word.

b y

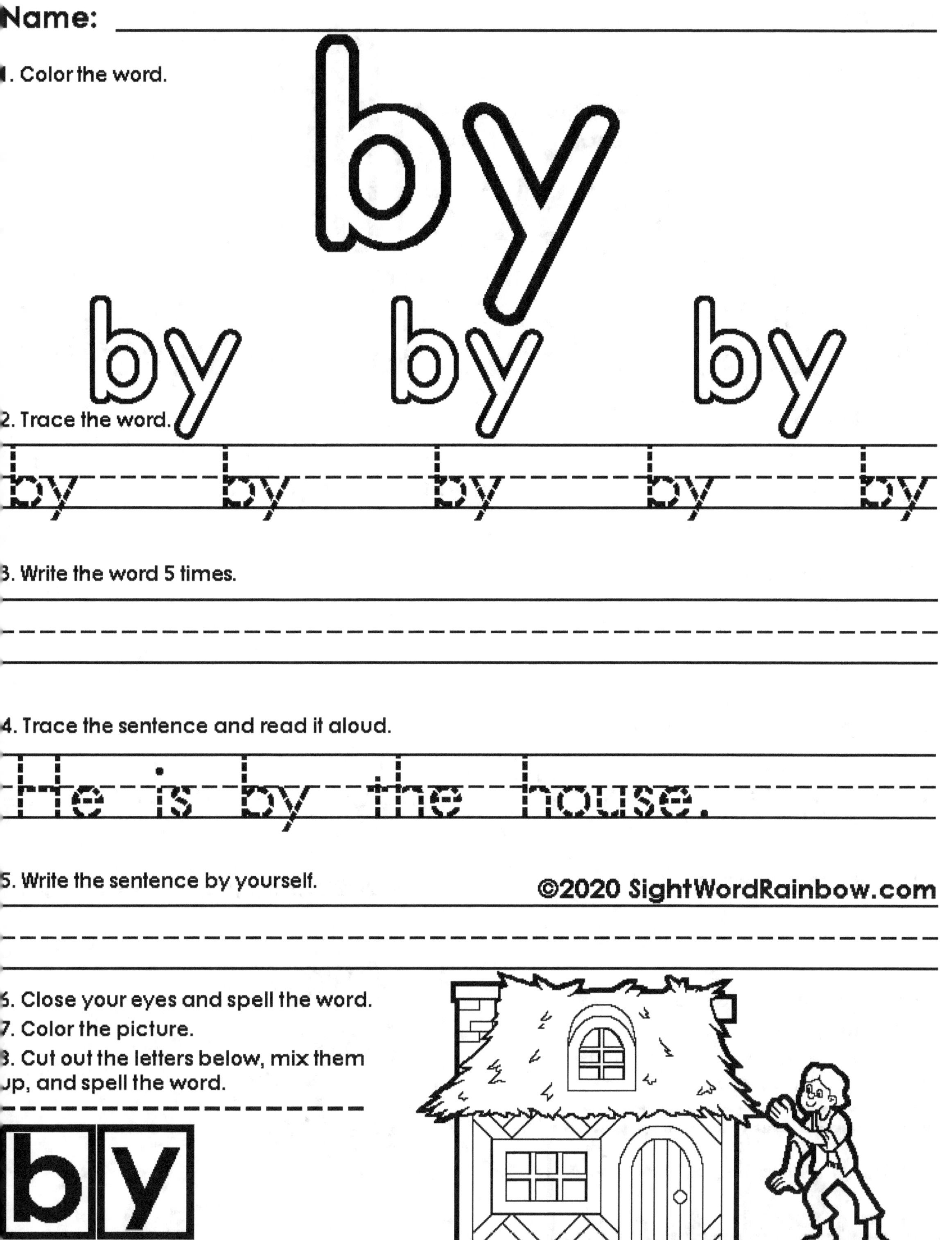

Name: _______________________

1. Color the word.

call

call   call   call

2. Trace the word.

call   call   call   call   call

3. Write the word 5 times.

4. Trace the sentence and read it aloud.

I will call my mom.

5. Write the sentence by yourself.

6. Close your eyes and spell the word.
7. Color the picture.
8. Cut out the letters below, mix them up, and spell the word.

c | a | l | l

Name: _______________________________

1. Color the word.

can

can   can   can

2. Trace the word.

can   can   can   can   can

3. Write the word 5 times.

4. Trace the sentence and read it aloud.

I can see a can.

5. Write the sentence by yourself.

©2020 SightWordRainbow.com

6. Close your eyes and spell the word.
7. Color the picture.
8. Cut out the letters below, mix them
up, and spell the word.

1. Color the word.

come

come   come

2. Trace the word.

come   come   come   come

3. Write the word 4 times.

4. Trace the sentence and read it aloud.

Can you come and play?

5. Write the sentence by yourself.

©2020 SightWordRainbow.com

6. Close your eyes and spell the word.
7. Color the picture.
8. Cut out the letters below, mix them up, and spell the word.

1. Color the word.

Could

could   could

2. Trace the word.

could   could   could   could

3. Write the word 4 times.

4. Trace the sentence and read it aloud.

We could make a castle.

5. Write the sentence by yourself.

©2020 SightWordRainbow.com

6. Close your eyes and spell the word.
7. Color the picture.
8. Cut out the letters below, mix them up, and spell the word.

c o u l d

Name: _______________________

1. Color the word.

day
day day day

2. Trace the word.

day day day day day

3. Write the word 5 times.

4. Trace the sentence and read it aloud.

It is not a hot day.

5. Write the sentence by yourself.

©2020 SightWordRainbow.com

6. Close your eyes and spell the word.
7. Color the picture.
8. Cut out the letters below, mix them up, and spell the word.

d a y

1. Color the word.

did

did did did did

2. Trace the word.

did did did did did

3. Write the word 5 times.

4. Trace the sentence and read it aloud.

Did you wash your hands?

5. Write the sentence by yourself.

6. Close your eyes and spell the word.

7. Color the picture.

8. Cut out the letters below, mix them up, and spell the word.

d i d

1. Color the word.

do

do do do do

2. Trace the word.

do do do do do

3. Write the word 5 times.

4. Trace the sentence and read it aloud.

Do you like pizza?

5. Write the sentence by yourself.

6. Close your eyes and spell the word.
7. Color the picture.
8. Cut out the letters below, mix them up, and spell the word.

d o

Name: ___________________________

1. Color the word.

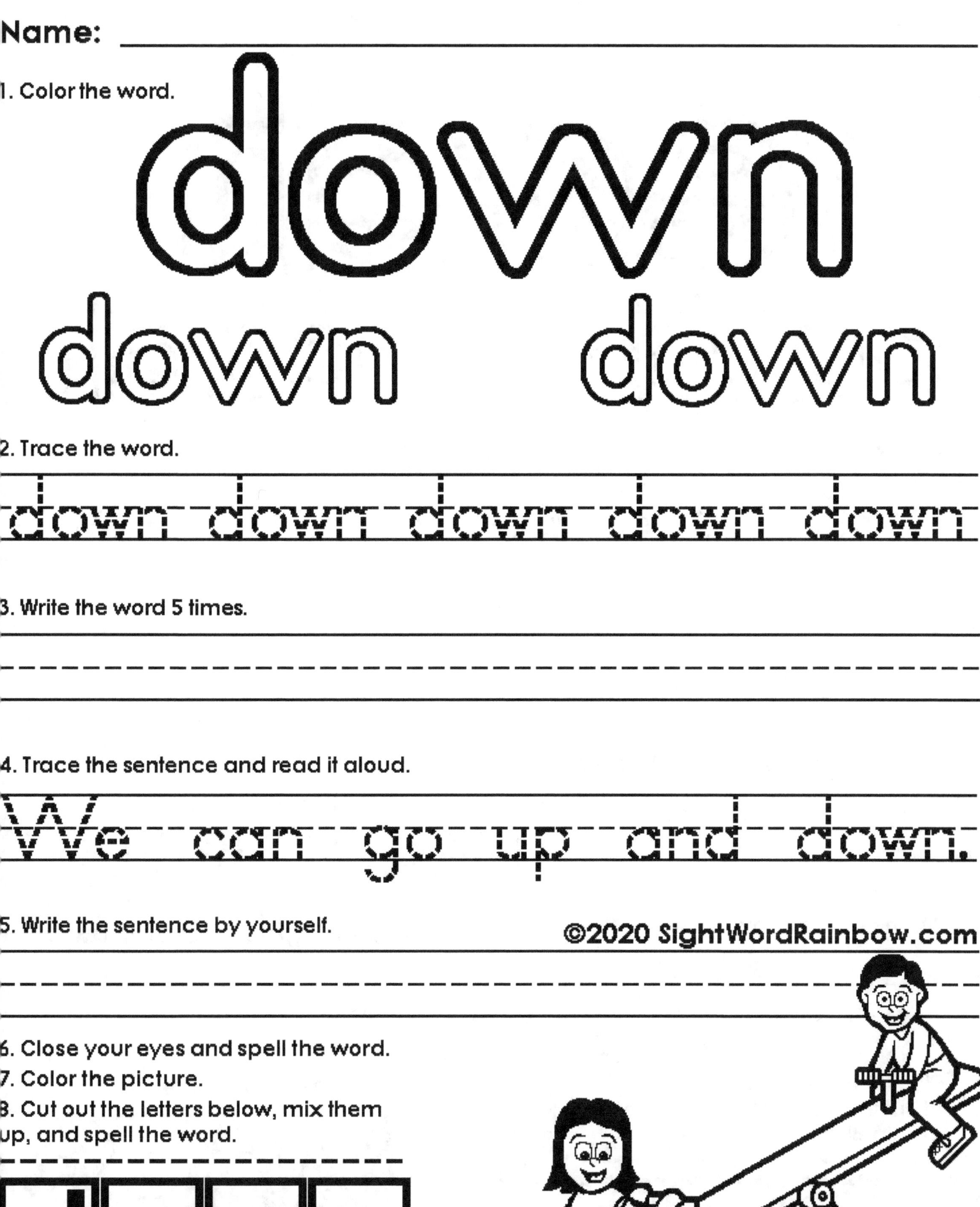

down

down   down

2. Trace the word.

down down down down down

3. Write the word 5 times.

4. Trace the sentence and read it aloud.

We can go up and down.

5. Write the sentence by yourself.

6. Close your eyes and spell the word.

7. Color the picture.

8. Cut out the letters below, mix them up, and spell the word.

d o w n

Name: ______________________________

1. Color the word.

each

each   each

2. Trace the word.

each each each each each

3. Write the word 5 times.

4. Trace the sentence and read it aloud.

Each one has 4 legs.

5. Write the sentence by yourself.

6. Close your eyes and spell the word.
7. Color the picture.
8. Cut out the letters below, mix them up, and spell the word.

| e | a | c | h |

Name: _______________________

1. Color the word.

find

find   find   find

2. Trace the word.

find find find find find

3. Write the word 5 times.

4. Trace the sentence and read it aloud.

I cannot find my shoes.

5. Write the sentence by yourself.

©2020 SightWordRainbow.com

6. Close your eyes and spell the word.

7. Color the picture.

8. Cut out the letters below, mix them up, and spell the word.

| f | i | n | d |

1. Color the word.

first

first first first

2. Trace the word.

first first first first first

3. Write the word 5 times.

4. Trace the sentence and read it aloud.

Can I dig in the sand first?

5. Write the sentence by yourself.

6. Close your eyes and spell the word.
7. Color the picture.
8. Cut out the letters below, mix them up, and spell the word.

f i r s t

1. Color the word.

2. Trace the word.

3. Write the word 5 times.

4. Trace the sentence and read it aloud.

5. Write the sentence by yourself.

©2020 SightWordRainbow.com

6. Close your eyes and spell the word.
7. Color the picture.
8. Cut out the letters below, mix them up, and spell the word.

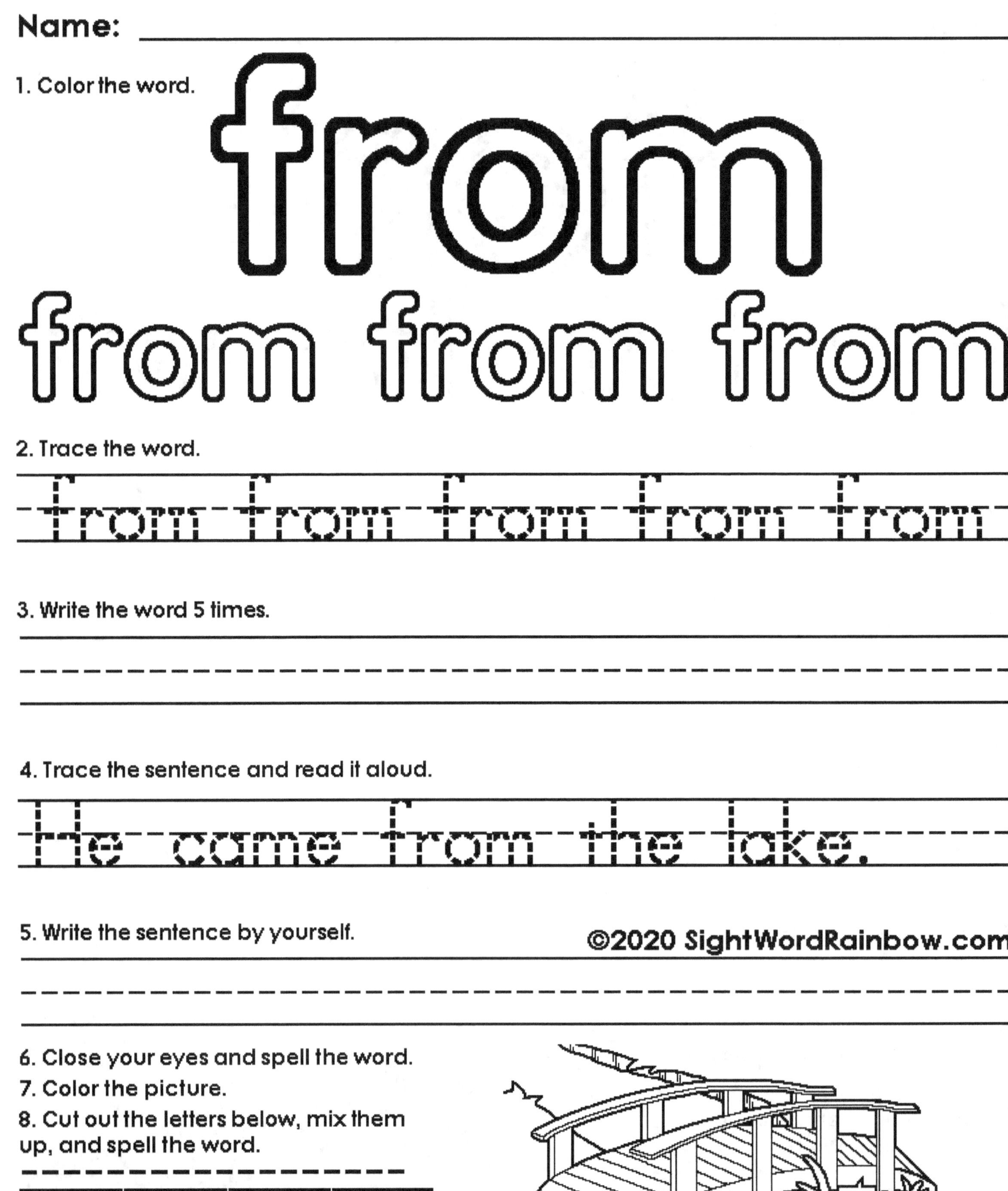

Name: ______________________

1. Color the word.

from

from from from

2. Trace the word.

from from from from from

3. Write the word 5 times.

4. Trace the sentence and read it aloud.

He came from the lake.

5. Write the sentence by yourself.

6. Close your eyes and spell the word.
7. Color the picture.
8. Cut out the letters below, mix them up, and spell the word.

f r o m

Name: _______________________

1. Color the word.

get

get get get

2. Trace the word.

get   get   get   get   get

3. Write the word 5 times.

4. Trace the sentence and read it aloud.

Can you get the keys?

5. Write the sentence by yourself.

©2020 SightWordRainbow.com

6. Close your eyes and spell the word.
7. Color the picture.
8. Cut out the letters below, mix them up, and spell the word.

g e t

Name: _______________________________

1. Color the word.

go

go   go   go   go

2. Trace the word.

go   go   go   go   go

3. Write the word 5 times.

4. Trace the sentence and read it aloud.

Go to bed!

5. Write the sentence by yourself.

6. Close your eyes and spell the word.
7. Color the picture.
8. Cut out the letters below, mix them up, and spell the word.

g o

1. Color the word.

had

had   had   had

2. Trace the word.

had   had   had   had   had

3. Write the word 5 times.

4. Trace the sentence and read it aloud.

She   had   a   big   castle.

5. Write the sentence by yourself.

©2020 SightWordRainbow.com

6. Close your eyes and spell the word.
7. Color the picture.
8. Cut out the letters below, mix them up, and spell the word.

had

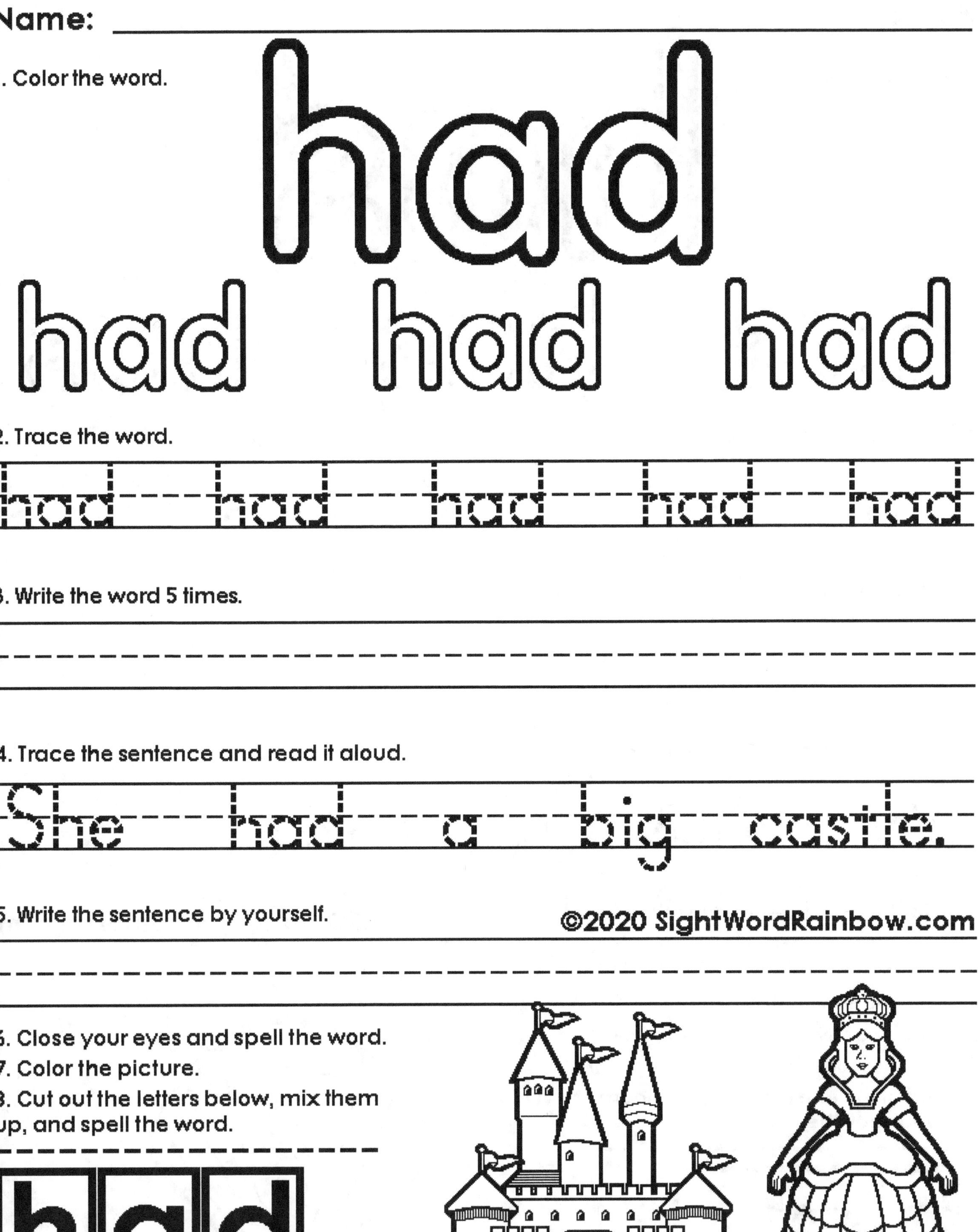

1. Color the word.

has

has has has

2. Trace the word.

has   has   has   has   has

3. Write the word 5 times.

4. Trace the sentence and read it aloud.

She   has   a   shell.

5. Write the sentence by yourself.

©2020 SightWordRainbow.com

6. Close your eyes and spell the word.
7. Color the picture.
8. Cut out the letters below, mix them up, and spell the word.

1. Color the word.

2. Trace the word.

3. Write the word 5 times.

4. Trace the sentence and read it aloud.

5. Write the sentence by yourself.

©2020 SightWordRainbow.com

6. Close your eyes and spell the word.
7. Color the picture.
8. Cut out the letters below, mix them
up, and spell the word.

1. Color the word.

he

he   he   he   he

2. Trace the word.

he   he   he   he   he

3. Write the word 5 times.

4. Trace the sentence and read it aloud.

He can see it.

5. Write the sentence by yourself.

6. Close your eyes and spell the word.
7. Color the picture.
8. Cut out the letters below, mix them up, and spell the word.

h e

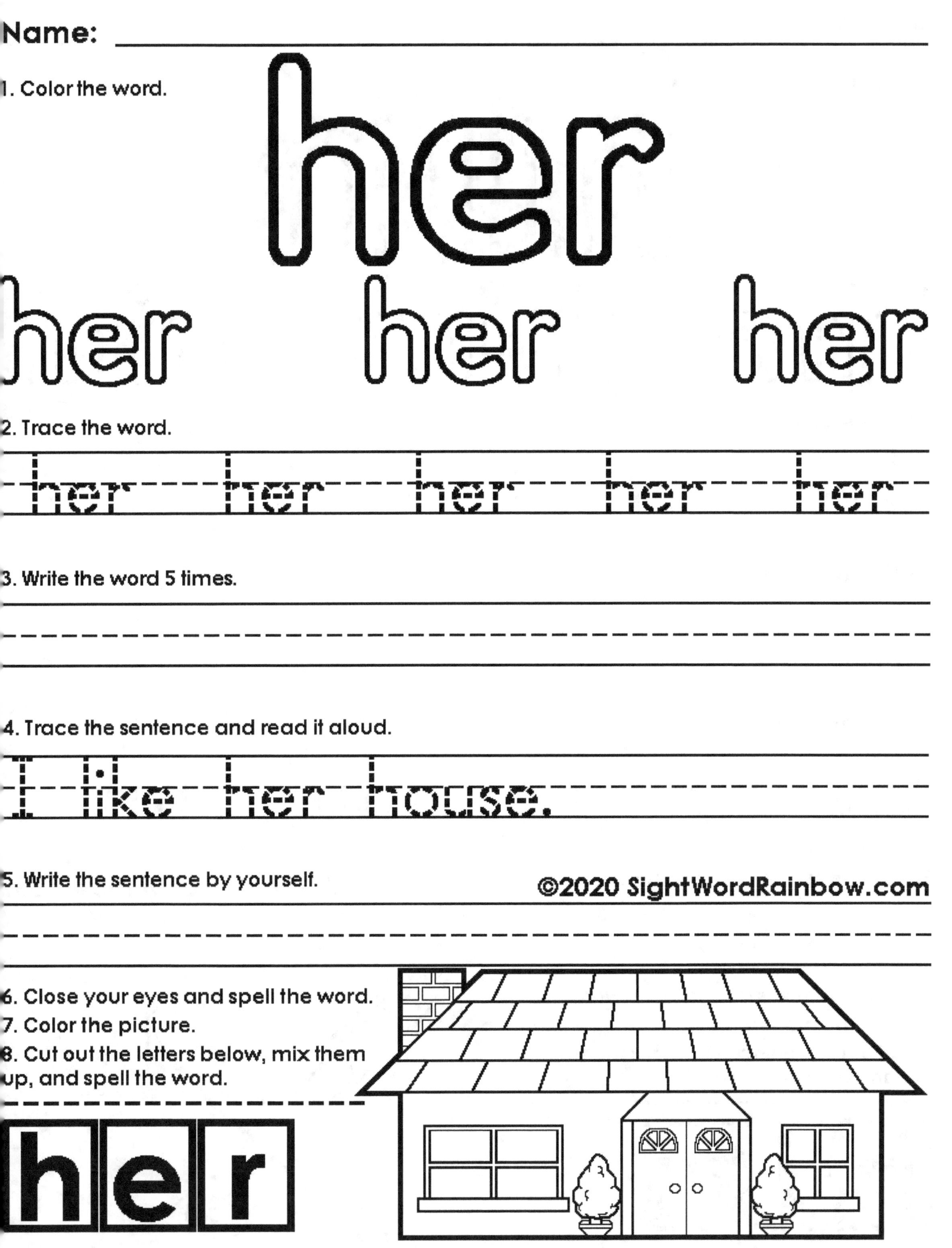

Name:

1. Color the word.

her

her   her   her

2. Trace the word.

her   her   her   her   her

3. Write the word 5 times.

4. Trace the sentence and read it aloud.

I like her house.

5. Write the sentence by yourself.

©2020 SightWordRainbow.com

6. Close your eyes and spell the word.
7. Color the picture.
8. Cut out the letters below, mix them up, and spell the word.

h e r

1. Color the word.

him

him **him** **him**

2. Trace the word.

him him him him him

3. Write the word 5 times.

4. Trace the sentence and read it aloud.

Get a pen for him.

5. Write the sentence by yourself.

6. Close your eyes and spell the word.

7. Color the picture.

8. Cut out the letters below, mix them up, and spell the word.

h i m

1. Color the word.

his

his his his

2. Trace the word.

his his his his his

3. Write the word 5 times.

4. Trace the sentence and read it aloud.

I like his cake.

5. Write the sentence by yourself.

©2020 SightWordRainbow.com

6. Close your eyes and spell the word.

7. Color the picture.

8. Cut out the letters below, mix them up, and spell the word.

h i s

Name: ___________________________

1. Color the word.

how

how how how

2. Trace the word.

how how how how how

3. Write the word 5 times.

4. Trace the sentence and read it aloud.

I like how you sing.

5. Write the sentence by yourself.

6. Close your eyes and spell the word.
7. Color the picture.
8. Cut out the letters below, mix them up, and spell the word.

how

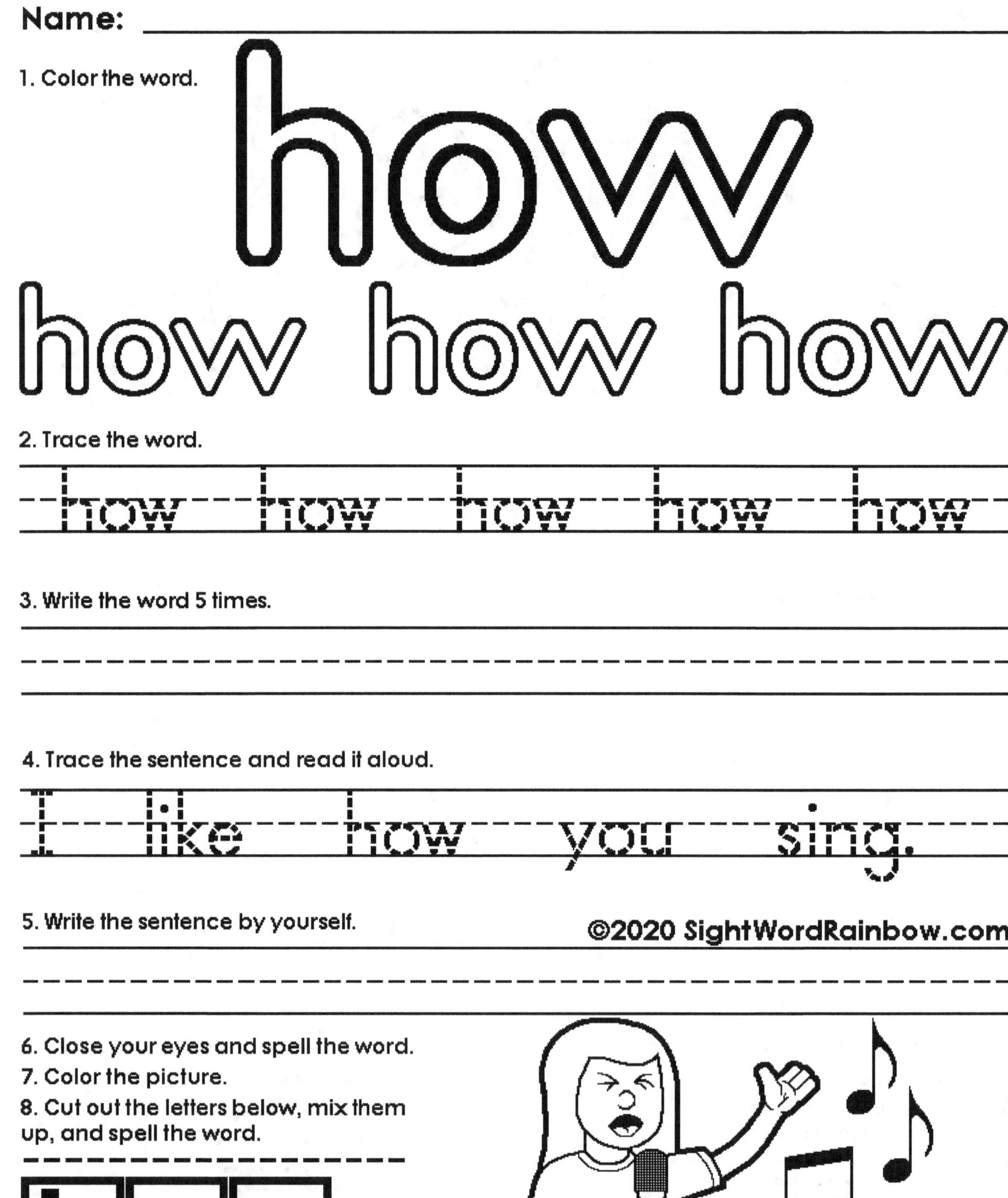

1. Color the word.

I

I   I   I   I

2. Trace the word.

I   I   I   I   I

3. Write the word 5 times.

4. Trace the sentence and read it aloud.

I run.

5. Write the sentence by yourself.

6. Close your eyes and spell the word.

7. Color the picture.

1. Color the word.

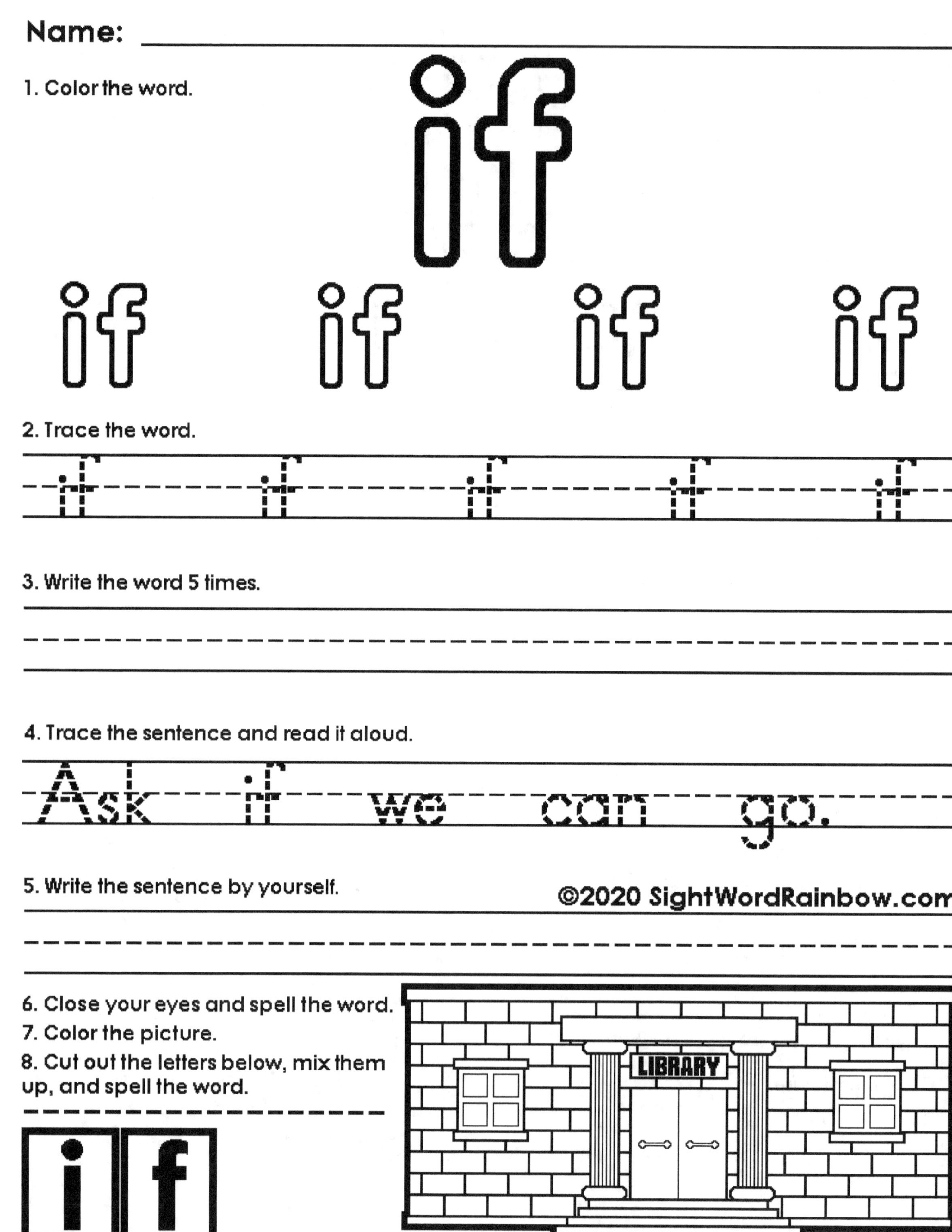

if

if   if   if   if

2. Trace the word.

if   if   if   if   if

3. Write the word 5 times.

4. Trace the sentence and read it aloud.

Ask if we can go.

5. Write the sentence by yourself.

©2020 SightWordRainbow.com

6. Close your eyes and spell the word.
7. Color the picture.
8. Cut out the letters below, mix them up, and spell the word.

i f

Name: _______________________

1. Color the word.

in

in   in   in   in

2. Trace the word.

in   in   in   in   in

3. Write the word 5 times.

4. Trace the sentence and read it aloud.

The rat is in the bag.

5. Write the sentence by yourself.

6. Close your eyes and spell the word.

7. Color the picture.

8. Cut out the letters below, mix them up, and spell the word.

i n

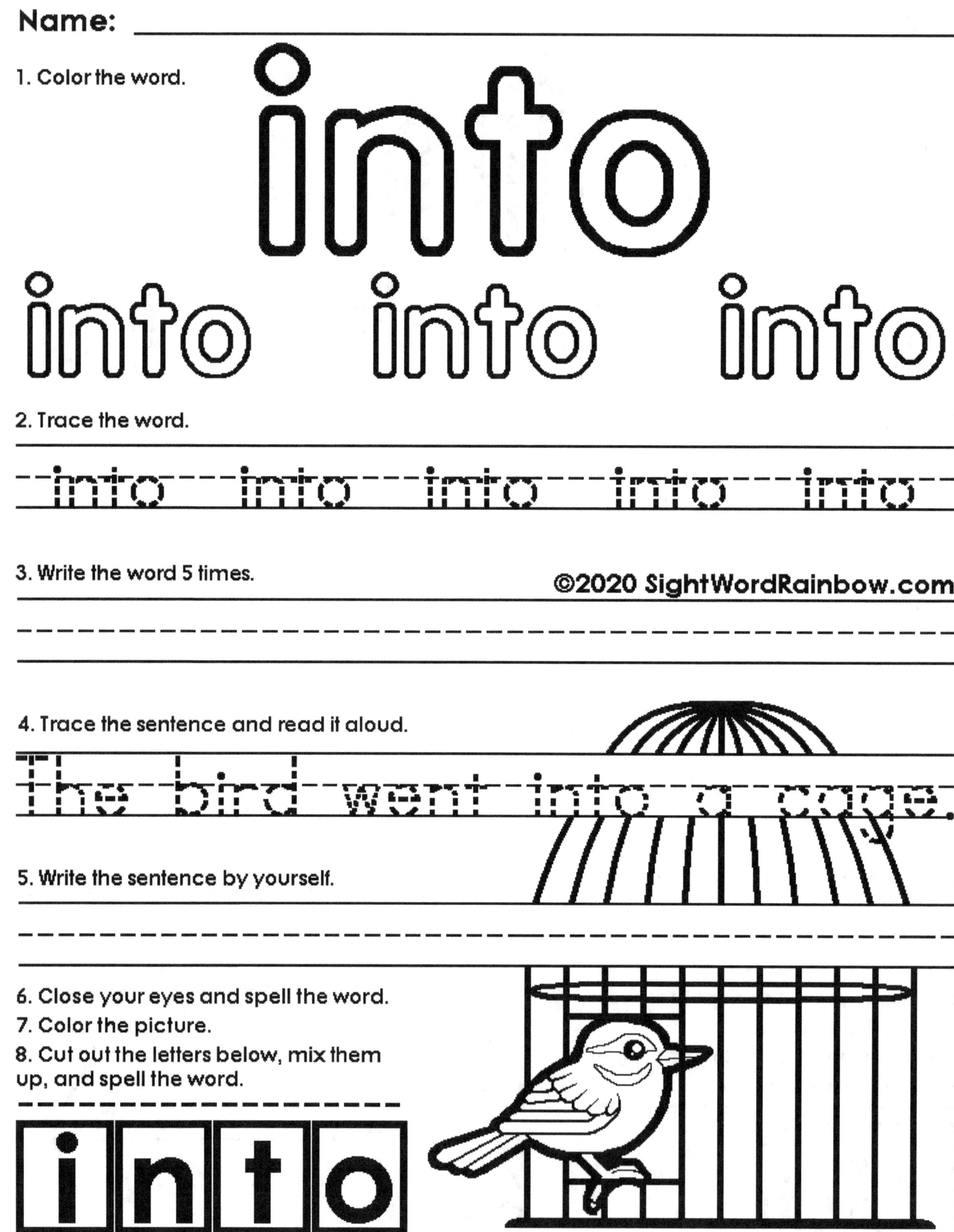

Name: _______________________

1. Color the word.

into

into into into

2. Trace the word.

into into into into into

3. Write the word 5 times.

©2020 SightWordRainbow.com

4. Trace the sentence and read it aloud.

The bird went into a cage.

5. Write the sentence by yourself.

6. Close your eyes and spell the word.
7. Color the picture.
8. Cut out the letters below, mix them up, and spell the word.

into

Name:

1. Color the word.

is

is   is   is   is

2. Trace the word.

is   is   is   is   is

3. Write the word 5 times.

4. Trace the sentence and read it aloud.

It is my hat.

5. Write the sentence by yourself.

©2020 SightWordRainbow.com

6. Close your eyes and spell the word.
7. Color the picture.
8. Cut out the letters below, mix them up, and spell the word.

i s

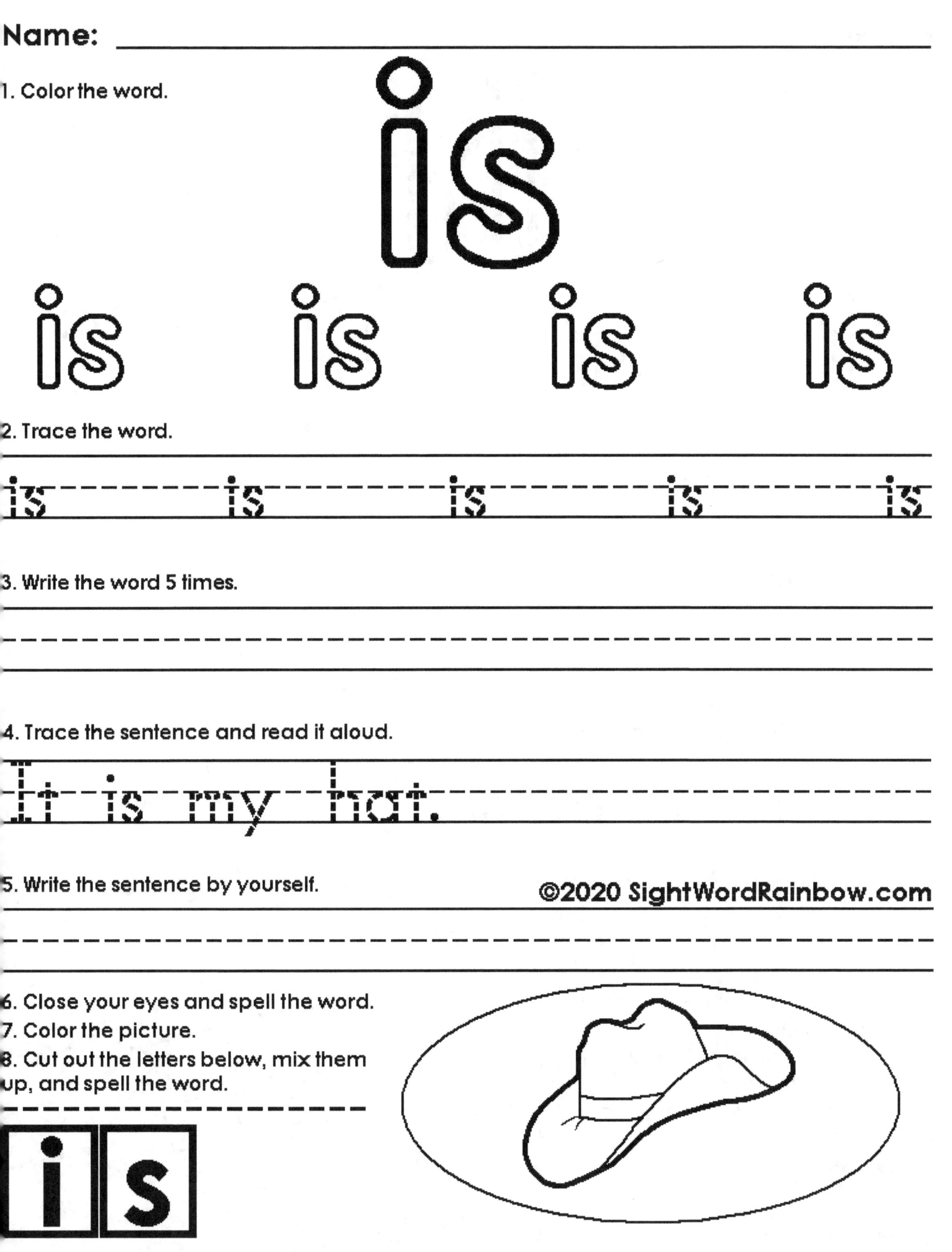

Name: ___________________________________

1. Color the word.

it

it   it   it   it

2. Trace the word.

it   it   it   it   it

3. Write the word 5 times.

4. Trace the sentence and read it aloud.

Is it a house?

5. Write the sentence by yourself.

6. Close your eyes and spell the word.
7. Color the picture.
8. Cut out the letters below, mix them up, and spell the word.

i t

1. Color the word.

its

its its its its

2. Trace the word.

its   its   its   its   its

3. Write the word 5 times.

4. Trace the sentence and read it aloud.

Look at its fin!

5. Write the sentence by yourself.

6. Close your eyes and spell the word.

7. Color the picture.

8. Cut out the letters below, mix them up, and spell the word.

i t s

1. Color the word.

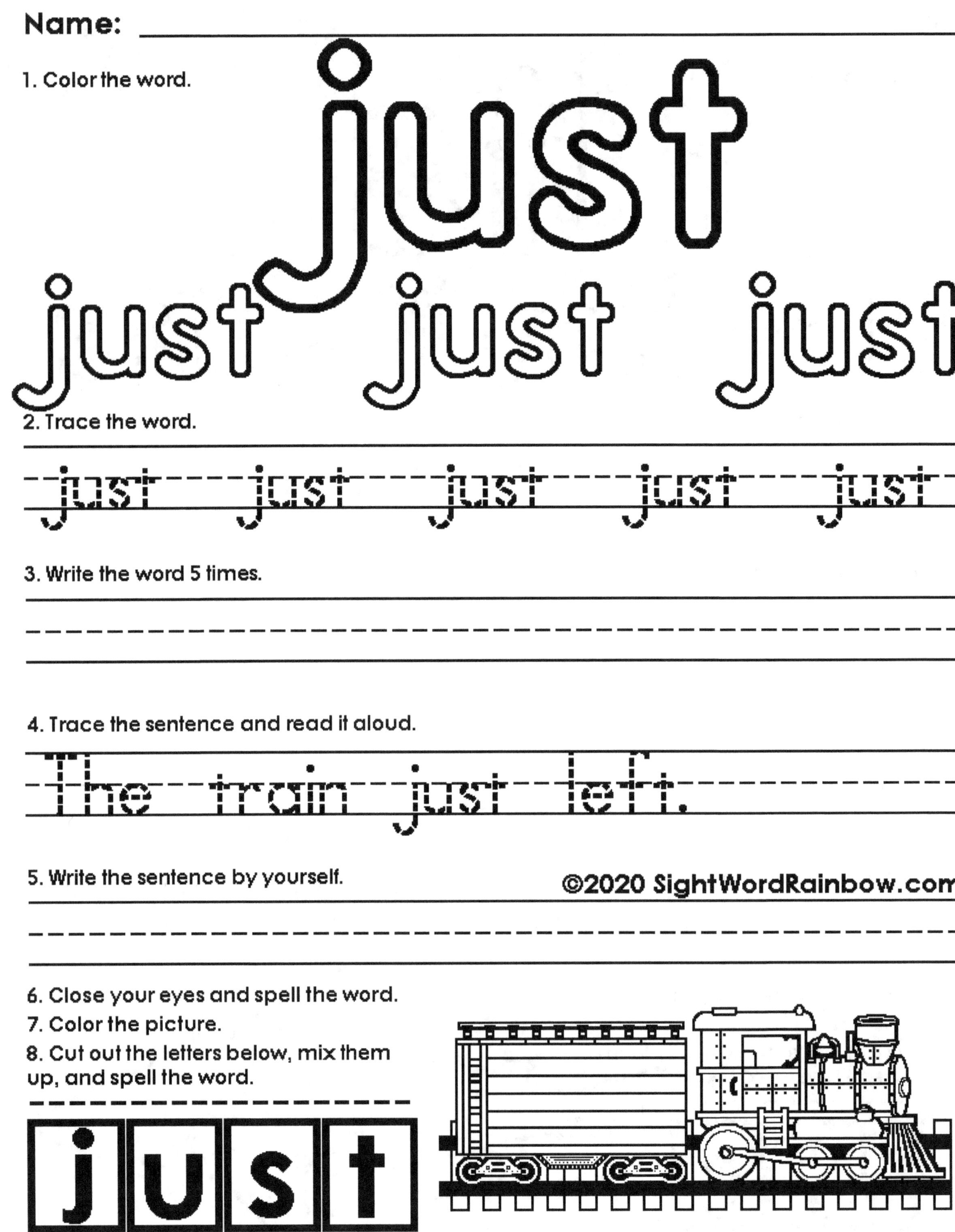

2. Trace the word.

just just just just just

3. Write the word 5 times.

4. Trace the sentence and read it aloud.

The train just left.

5. Write the sentence by yourself.

©2020 SightWordRainbow.com

6. Close your eyes and spell the word.
7. Color the picture.
8. Cut out the letters below, mix them up, and spell the word.

j u s t

1. Color the word.

know

know   know

2. Trace the word.

know   know   know   know

3. Write the word 4 times.

4. Trace the sentence and read it aloud.

We know how to read!

5. Write the sentence by yourself.

©2020 SightWordRainbow.com

6. Close your eyes and spell the word.

7. Color the picture.

8. Cut out the letters below, mix them up, and spell the word.

1. Color the word.

like
like like like like

2. Trace the word.

like   like   like   like   like

3. Write the word 5 times.

4. Trace the sentence and read it aloud.

Do you like my toy?

5. Write the sentence by yourself.

6. Close your eyes and spell the word.
7. Color the picture.
8. Cut out the letters below, mix them up, and spell the word.

l i k e

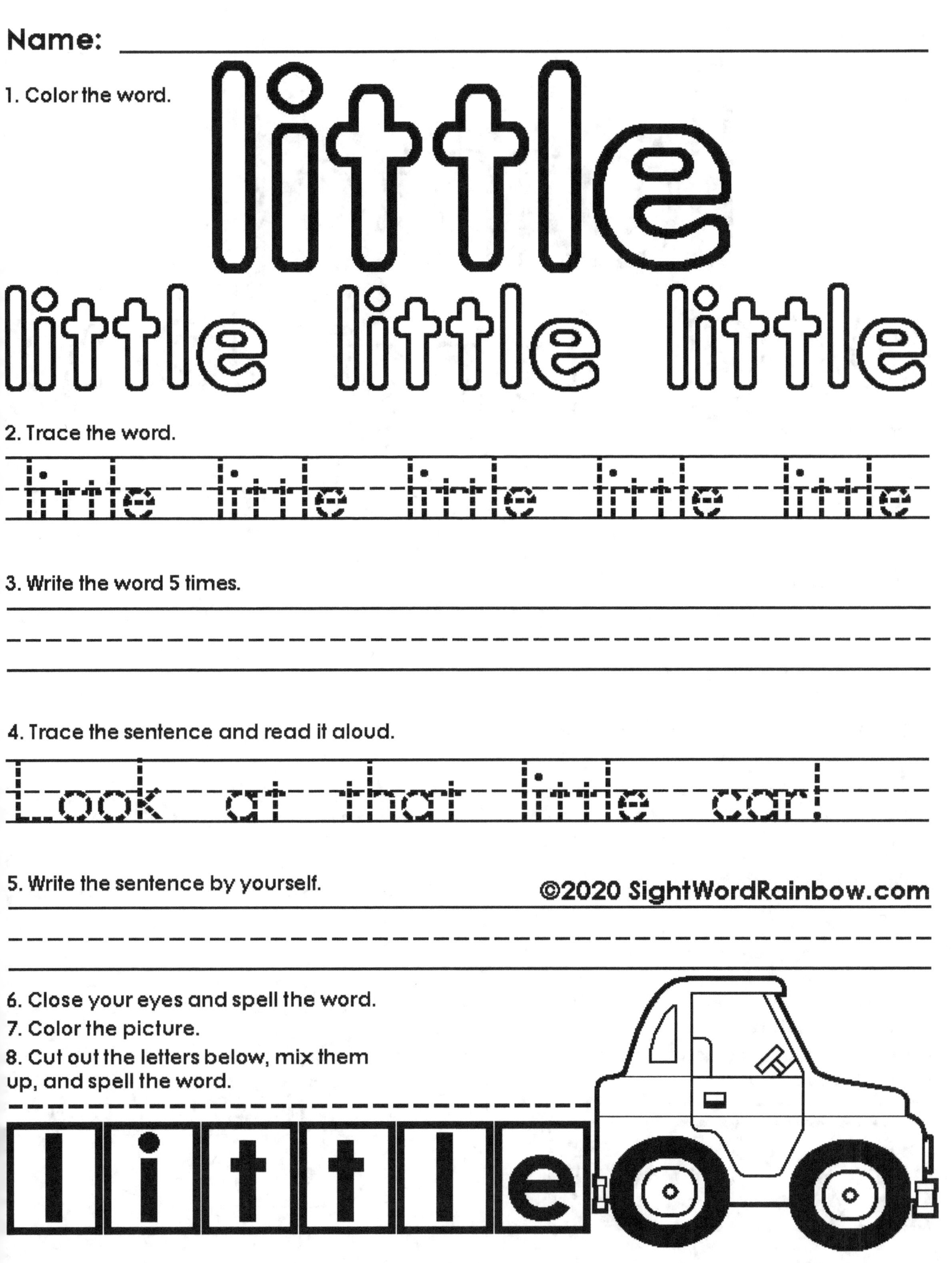

Name:
1. Color the word.
little
little little little
2. Trace the word.
little little little little little
3. Write the word 5 times.
4. Trace the sentence and read it aloud.
Look at that little car!
5. Write the sentence by yourself.
©2020 SightWordRainbow.com
6. Close your eyes and spell the word.
7. Color the picture.
8. Cut out the letters below, mix them up, and spell the word.
l i t t l e

1. Color the word.

long
long long long

2. Trace the word.

long long long long long

3. Write the word 5 times.

4. Trace the sentence and read it aloud.

That is a long snake.

5. Write the sentence by yourself.

©2020 SightWordRainbow.com

6. Close your eyes and spell the word.
7. Color the picture.
8. Cut out the letters below, mix them up, and spell the word.

l o n g

1. Color the word.

look

look look look

2. Trace the word.

look look look look look

3. Write the word 5 times.

4. Trace the sentence and read it aloud.

Look at that!

5. Write the sentence by yourself.

©2020 SightWordRainbow.com

6. Close your eyes and spell the word.
7. Color the picture.
8. Cut out the letters below, mix them up, and spell the word.

l o o k

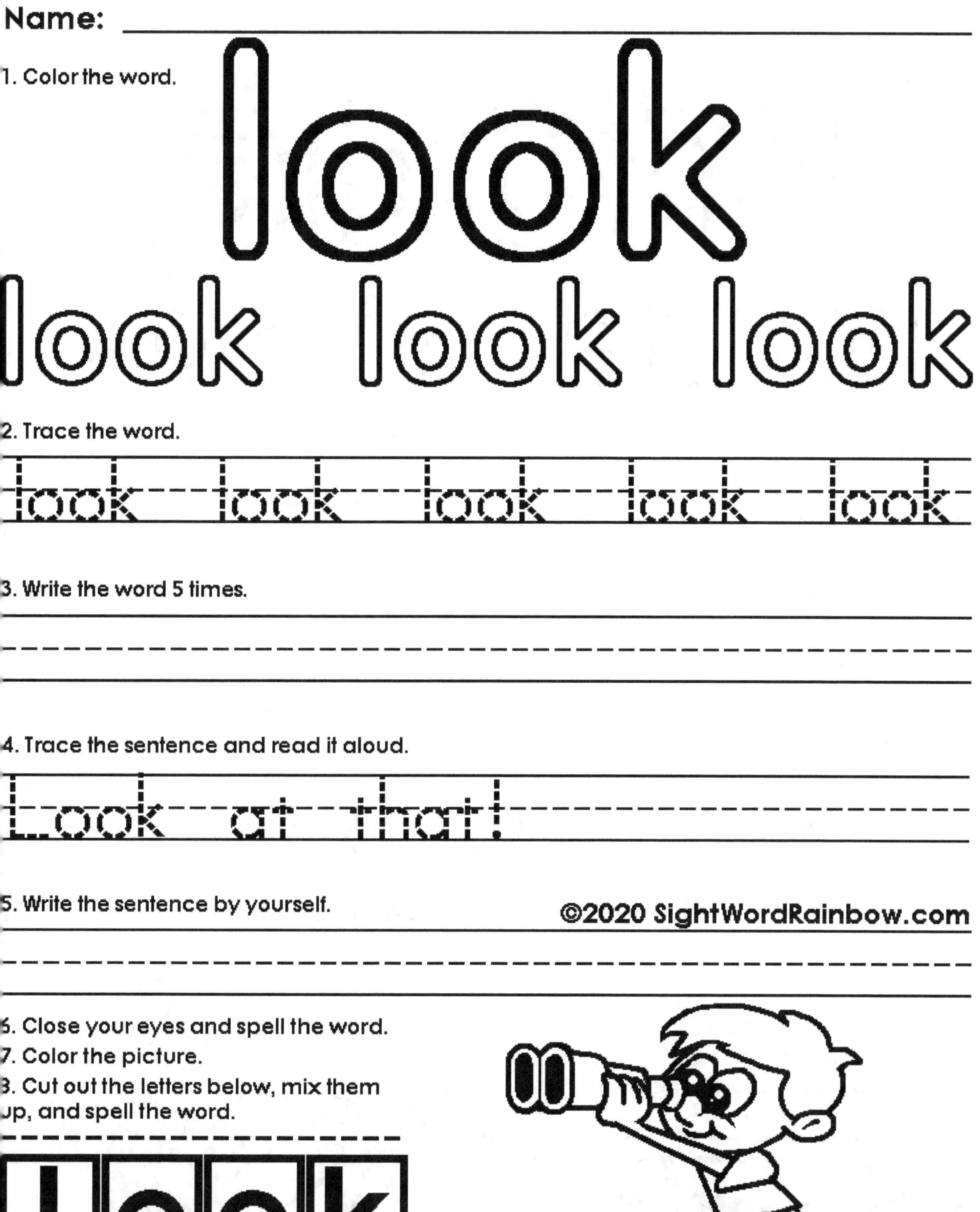

1. Color the word.

made
made   made

2. Trace the word.

made   made   made   made

3. Write the word 4 times.

4. Trace the sentence and read it aloud.

I made it for you.

5. Write the sentence by yourself.

©2020 SightWordRainbow.com

6. Close your eyes and spell the word.
7. Color the picture.
8. Cut out the letters below, mix them up, and spell the word.

m a d e

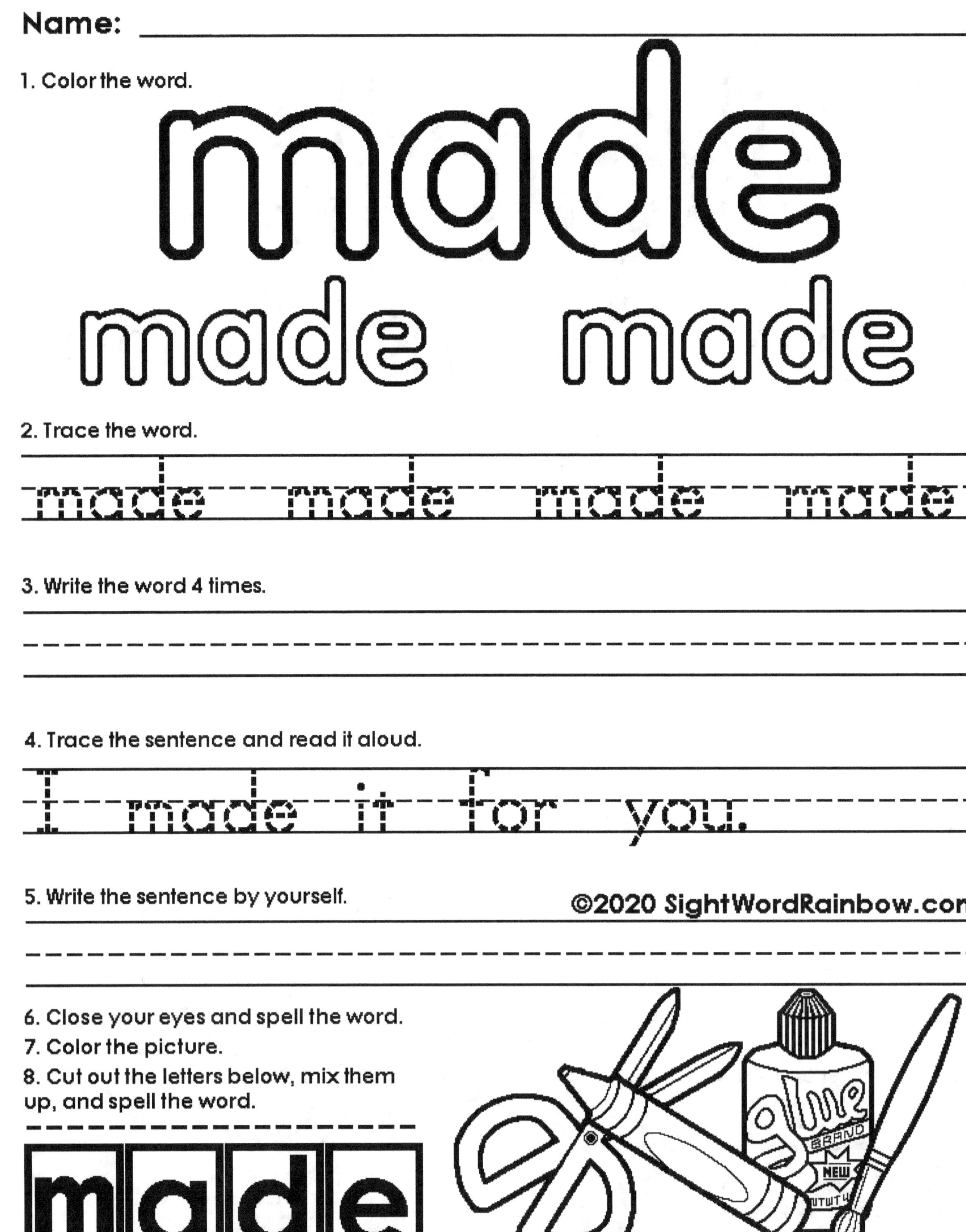

1. Color the word.

make
make   make

2. Trace the word.

make   make   make   make

3. Write the word 4 times.

____

_ _ _ _ _ _ _ _ _ _ _ _ _ _ _ _ _

____

4. Trace the sentence and read it aloud.

You   make   me   happy!

5. Write the sentence by yourself.   ©2020 SightWordRainbow.com

____

_ _ _ _ _ _ _ _ _ _ _ _ _ _ _ _ _

6. Close your eyes and spell the word.
7. Color the picture.
8. Cut out the letters below, mix them
up, and spell the word.

- - - - - - - - - - - - - - - - -

Name: _______________________

1. Color the word.

many

many   many

2. Trace the word.

many   many   many   many

3. Write the word 4 times.

4. Trace the sentence and read it aloud.

I see so many forks.

5. Write the sentence by yourself.

6. Close your eyes and spell the word.

7. Color the picture.

8. Cut out the letters below, mix them up, and spell the word.

m a n y

1. Color the word.

Name: _______________________

1. Color the word.

2. Trace the word.

more more more more more

3. Write the word 5 times.

4. Trace the sentence and read it aloud.

May I have some more?

5. Write the sentence by yourself.

©2020 SightWordRainbow.com

6. Close your eyes and spell the word.
7. Color the picture.
8. Cut out the letters below, mix them
up, and spell the word.

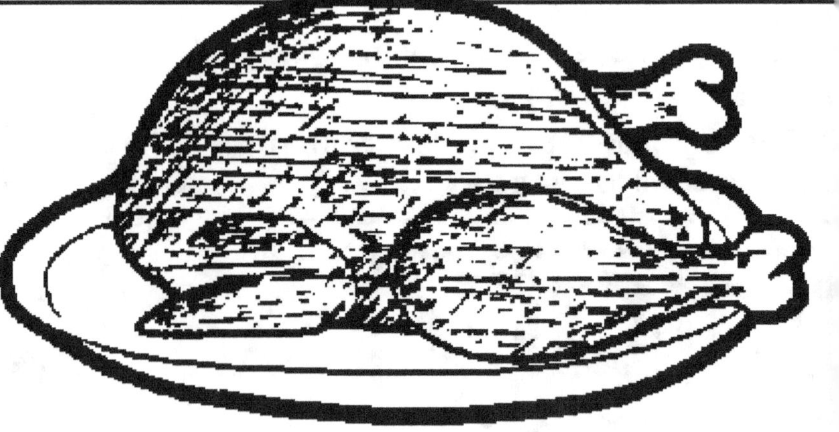

1. Color the word.

most

most   most

2. Trace the word.

most most most most most

3. Write the word 5 times.

4. Trace the sentence and read it aloud.

I love you the most.

5. Write the sentence by yourself.

©2020 SightWordRainbow.com

6. Close your eyes and spell the word.
7. Color the picture.
8. Cut out the letters below, mix them up, and spell the word.

Name: _______________________________

1. Color the word.

my

my   my   my

2. Trace the word.

my   my   my   my   my

3. Write the word 5 times.

4. Trace the sentence and read it aloud.

I   see   my   dog.

5. Write the sentence by yourself.

6. Close your eyes and spell the word.
7. Color the picture.
8. Cut out the letters below, mix them up, and spell the word.

m y

Name: _______________________________

1. Color the word.

no

no   no   no   no

2. Trace the word.

no   no   no   no   no

3. Write the word 5 times.

4. Trace the sentence and read it aloud.

My   mom   said   no!

5. Write the sentence by yourself.

6. Close your eyes and spell the word.
7. Color the picture.
8. Cut out the letters below, mix them up, and spell the word.

n o

Name: ______________________

1. Color the word.

not

not   not   not

2. Trace the word.

not   not   not   not   not

3. Write the word 5 times.

4. Trace the sentence and read it aloud.

I am not hot.

5. Write the sentence by yourself.

©2020 SightWordRainbow.com

6. Close your eyes and spell the word.
7. Color the picture.
8. Cut out the letters below, mix them up, and spell the word.

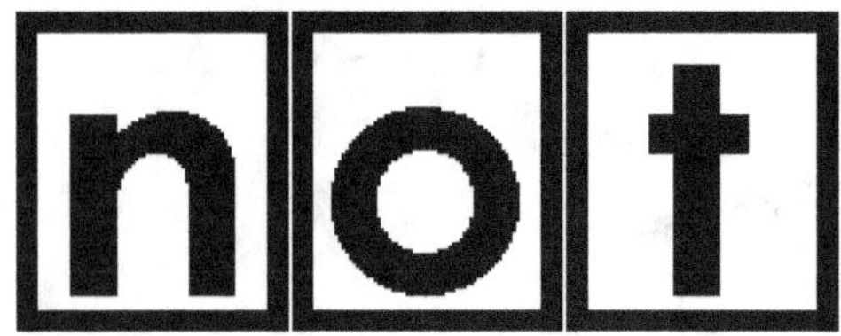

1. Color the word.

now

now now now

2. Trace the word.

now now now now now

3. Write the word 5 times.

4. Trace the sentence and read it aloud.

Now I can see you.

5. Write the sentence by yourself.

©2020 SightWordRainbow.com

6. Close your eyes and spell the word.
7. Color the picture.
8. Cut out the letters below, mix them up, and spell the word.

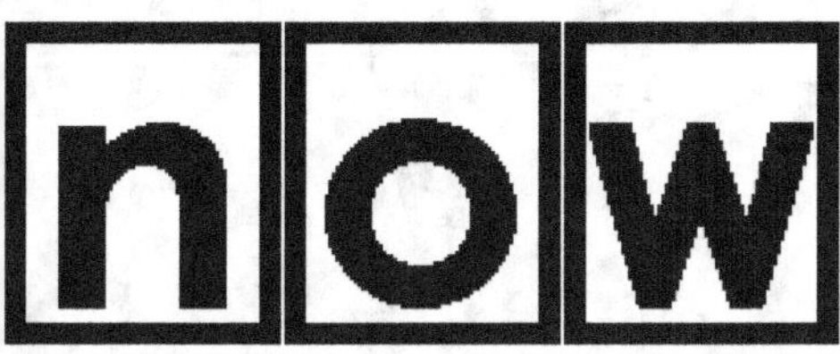

1. Color the word.

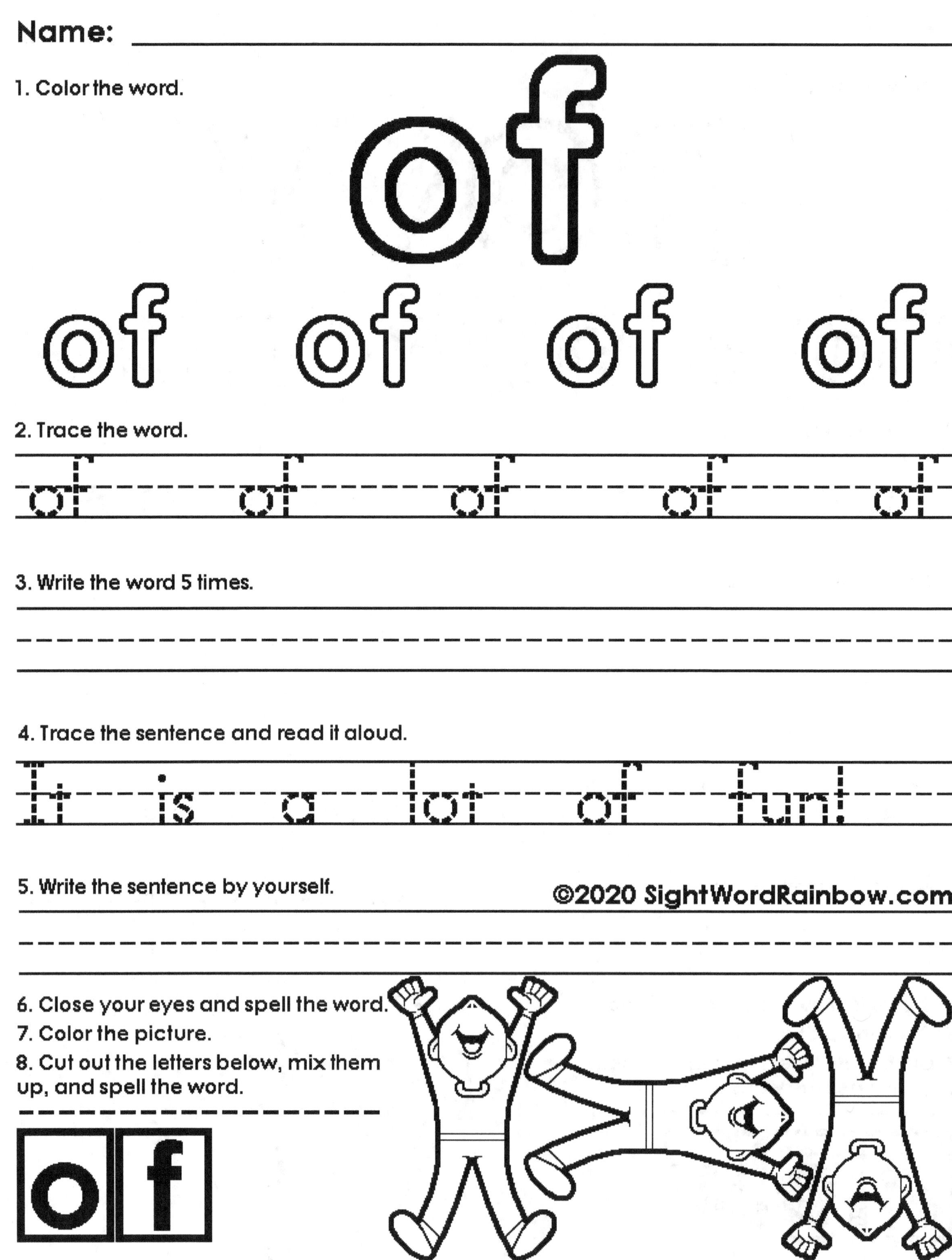

of
of of of of

2. Trace the word.

of   of   of   of   of

3. Write the word 5 times.

4. Trace the sentence and read it aloud.

It is a lot of fun!

5. Write the sentence by yourself.

©2020 SightWordRainbow.com

6. Close your eyes and spell the word.
7. Color the picture.
8. Cut out the letters below, mix them up, and spell the word.

o f

1. Color the word.

on

on on on on

2. Trace the word.

on   on   on   on   on

3. Write the word 5 times.

4. Trace the sentence and read it aloud.

My fork is on top.

5. Write the sentence by yourself.

©2020 SightWordRainbow.com

6. Close your eyes and spell the word.

7. Color the picture.

8. Cut out the letters below, mix them up, and spell the word.

o n

1. Color the word.

one

one   one   one

2. Trace the word.

one   one   one   one   one

3. Write the word 5 times.

4. Trace the sentence and read it aloud.

I can see one!

5. Write the sentence by yourself.

6. Close your eyes and spell the word.
7. Color the picture.
8. Cut out the letters below, mix them up, and spell the word.

o n e

1. Color the word.

only

only only only

2. Trace the word.

only only only only only

3. Write the word 5 times.

4. Trace the sentence and read it aloud.

It is only a snail.

5. Write the sentence by yourself.

©2020 SightWordRainbow.com

6. Close your eyes and spell the word.

7. Color the picture.

8. Cut out the letters below, mix them up, and spell the word.

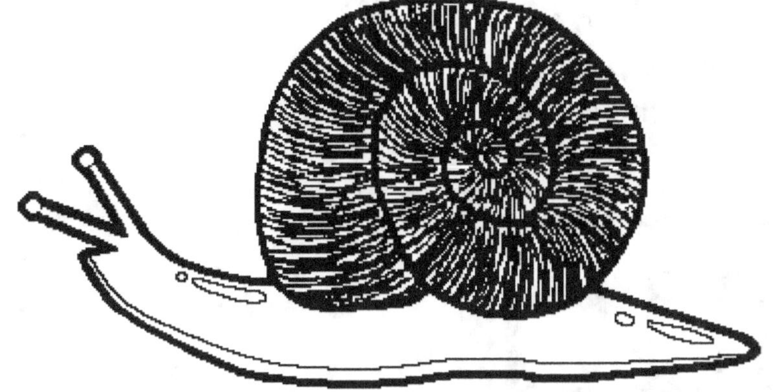

1. Color the word.

or

or   or   or   or

2. Trace the word.

or   or   or   or   or

3. Write the word 5 times.

4. Trace the sentence and read it aloud.

Do you want milk or soda?

5. Write the sentence by yourself.

6. Close your eyes and spell the word.
7. Color the picture.
8. Cut out the letters below, mix them up, and spell the word.

o r

1. Color the word.

other

other   other

2. Trace the word.

other   other   other   other

3. Write the word 4 times.

4. Trace the sentence and read it aloud.

Can I use the other cup?

5. Write the sentence by yourself.

©2020 SightWordRainbow.com

6. Close your eyes and spell the word.
7. Color the picture.
8. Cut out the letters below, mix them up, and spell the word.

o t h e r

1. Color the word.

out

out   out   out

2. Trace the word.

out   out   out   out   out

3. Write the word 5 times.

4. Trace the sentence and read it aloud.

I am out in the rain.

5. Write the sentence by yourself.

©2020 SightWordRainbow.com

6. Close your eyes and spell the word.
7. Color the picture.
8. Cut out the letters below, mix them up, and spell the word.

o u t

1. Color the word.

over

over over over

2. Trace the word.

over over over over over

3. Write the word 5 times.

4. Trace the sentence and read it aloud.

The concert is over.

5. Write the sentence by yourself.

6. Close your eyes and spell the word.
7. Color the picture.
8. Cut out the letters below, mix them up, and spell the word.

o v e r

Name: _______________________

1. Color the word.

said

said said said

2. Trace the word.

said said said said said

3. Write the word 5 times.

4. Trace the sentence and read it aloud.

Dad said I can go.

5. Write the sentence by yourself.

6. Close your eyes and spell the word.
7. Color the picture.
8. Cut out the letters below, mix them up, and spell the word.

s a i d

1. Color the word.

see

see   see   see

2. Trace the word.

see   see   see   see   see

3. Write the word 5 times.

4. Trace the sentence and read it aloud.

You   cannot   see   me!

5. Write the sentence by yourself.

©2020 SightWordRainbow.com

6. Close your eyes and spell the word.

7. Color the picture.

8. Cut out the letters below, mix them up, and spell the word.

1. Color the word.

she

she she she

2. Trace the word.

she she she she she

3. Write the word 5 times.

4. Trace the sentence and read it aloud.

She has the ball.

5. Write the sentence by yourself.

©2020 SightWordRainbow.com

6. Close your eyes and spell the word.

7. Color the picture.

8. Cut out the letters below, mix them up, and spell the word.

s h e

1. Color the word.

SO

SO   SO   SO   SO

2. Trace the word.

SO   SO   SO   SO   SO

3. Write the word 5 times.

4. Trace the sentence and read it aloud.

He is so sad.

5. Write the sentence by yourself.

6. Close your eyes and spell the word.

7. Color the picture.

8. Cut out the letters below, mix them up, and spell the word.

S O

1. Color the word.

some

some   some

2. Trace the word.

some some some some some

3. Write the word 5 times.

4. Trace the sentence and read it aloud.

I   see   some   cats.

5. Write the sentence by yourself.

©2020 SightWordRainbow.com

6. Close your eyes and spell the word.
7. Color the picture.
8. Cut out the letters below, mix them up, and spell the word.

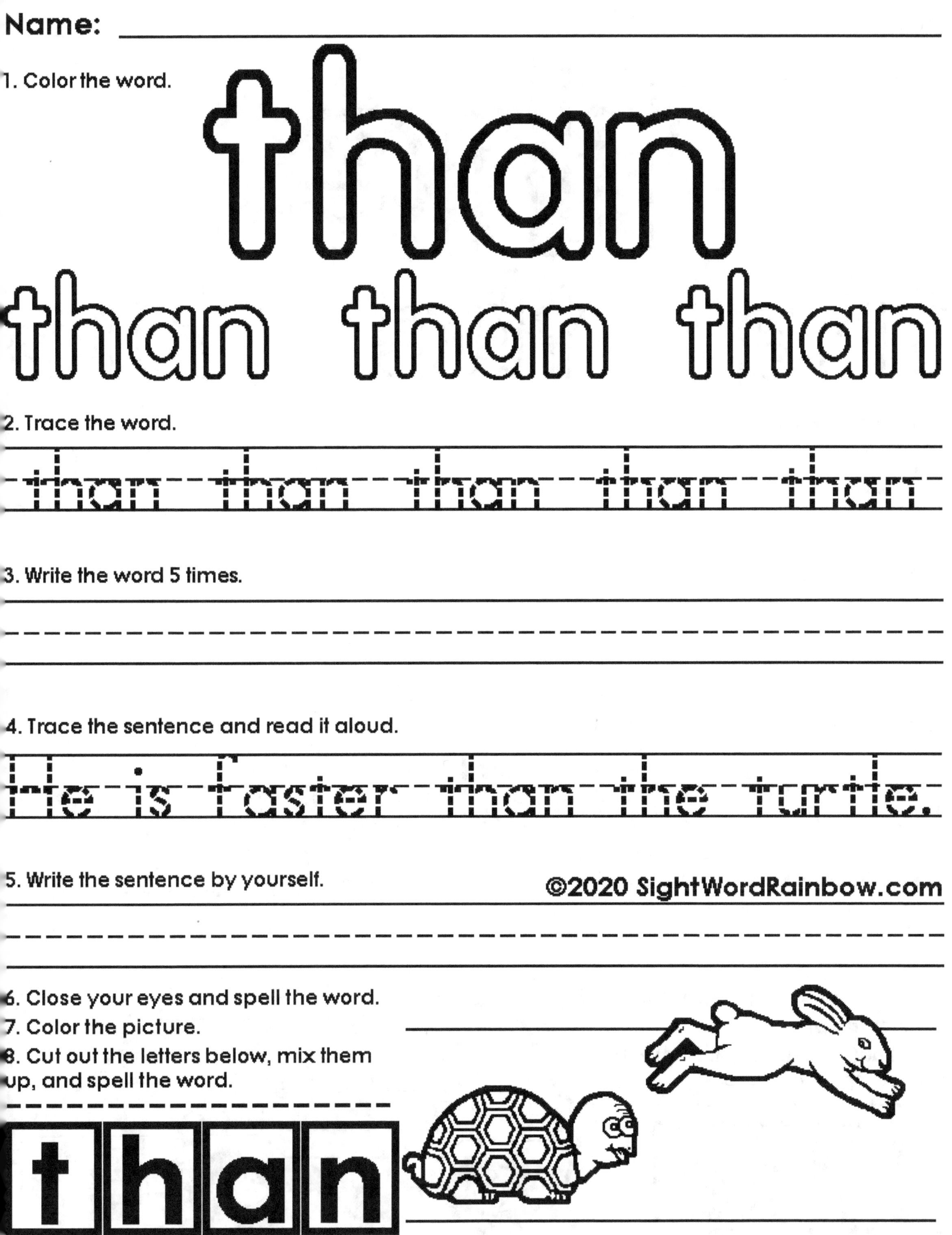

Name: ___________________________

1. Color the word.

than

than than than

2. Trace the word.

than than than than than

3. Write the word 5 times.

4. Trace the sentence and read it aloud.

He is faster than the turtle.

5. Write the sentence by yourself.

©2020 SightWordRainbow.com

6. Close your eyes and spell the word.
7. Color the picture.
8. Cut out the letters below, mix them up, and spell the word.

t h a n

Name: _______________

1. Color the word.

the
the   the   the

2. Trace the word.

the   the   the   the   the

3. Write the word 5 times.

4. Trace the sentence and read it aloud.

I can see the red van.

5. Write the sentence by yourself.

©2020 SightWordRainbow.com

6. Close your eyes and spell the word.
7. Color the picture.
8. Cut out the letters below, mix them up, and spell the word.

t h e

1234

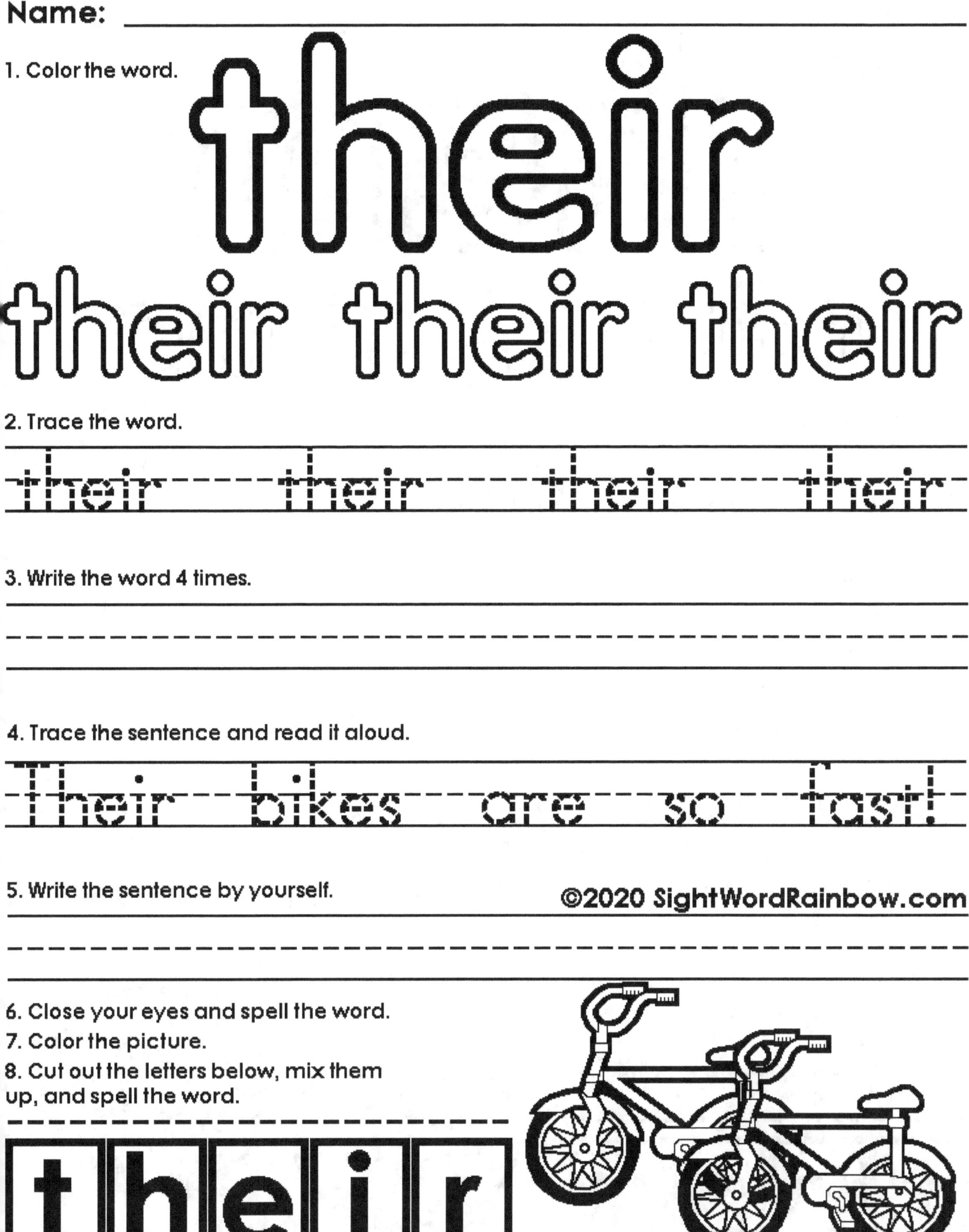

Name: _______________________________

1. Color the word.

their
their their their

2. Trace the word.

their their their their

3. Write the word 4 times.

4. Trace the sentence and read it aloud.

Their bikes are so fast!

5. Write the sentence by yourself.

©2020 SightWordRainbow.com

6. Close your eyes and spell the word.
7. Color the picture.
8. Cut out the letters below, mix them up, and spell the word.

t h e i r

1. Color the word.

them

them   them

2. Trace the word.

them them them them them

3. Write the word 5 times.

4. Trace the sentence and read it aloud.

Let them have a donut.

5. Write the sentence by yourself.

©2020 SightWordRainbow.com

6. Close your eyes and spell the word.
7. Color the picture.
8. Cut out the letters below, mix them up, and spell the word.

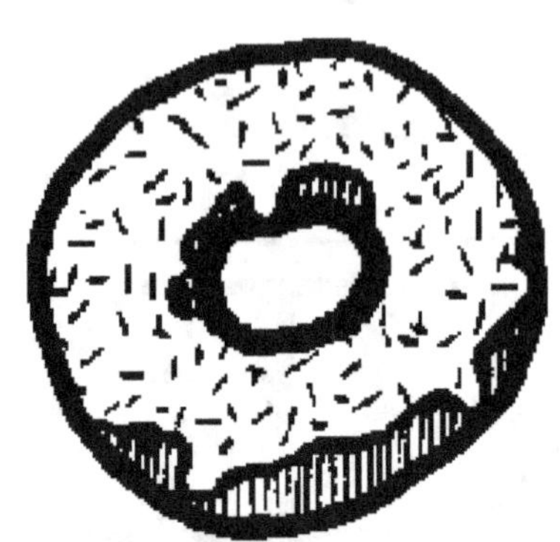

1. Color the word.

then

then then then

2. Trace the word.

then then then then then

3. Write the word 5 times.

4. Trace the sentence and read it aloud.

Then I saw a dragon!

5. Write the sentence by yourself.

©2020 SightWordRainbow.com

6. Close your eyes and spell the word.
7. Color the picture.
8. Cut out the letters below, mix them up, and spell the word.

t h e n

Name:
1. Color the word.
there
there   there
2. Trace the word.
there   there   there   there
3. Write the word 4 times.
4. Trace the sentence and read it aloud.
How do I get there?
5. Write the sentence by yourself.
©2020 SightWordRainbow.com
6. Close your eyes and spell the word.
7. Color the picture.
8. Cut out the letters below, mix them up, and spell the word.
t h e r e
STOP
STOP

1. Color the word.

these
these   these

2. Trace the word.

these   these   these   these

3. Write the word 4 times.

4. Trace the sentence and read it aloud.

Do you like these animals?

5. Write the sentence by yourself.

©2020 SightWordRainbow.com

6. Close your eyes and spell the word.
7. Color the picture.
8. Cut out the letters below, mix them
up, and spell the word.

1. Color the word.

they

they they they

2. Trace the word.

they they they they they

3. Write the word 5 times.

4. Trace the sentence and read it aloud.

They were so happy.

5. Write the sentence by yourself.

6. Close your eyes and spell the word.

7. Color the picture.

8. Cut out the letters below, mix them up, and spell the word.

t h e y

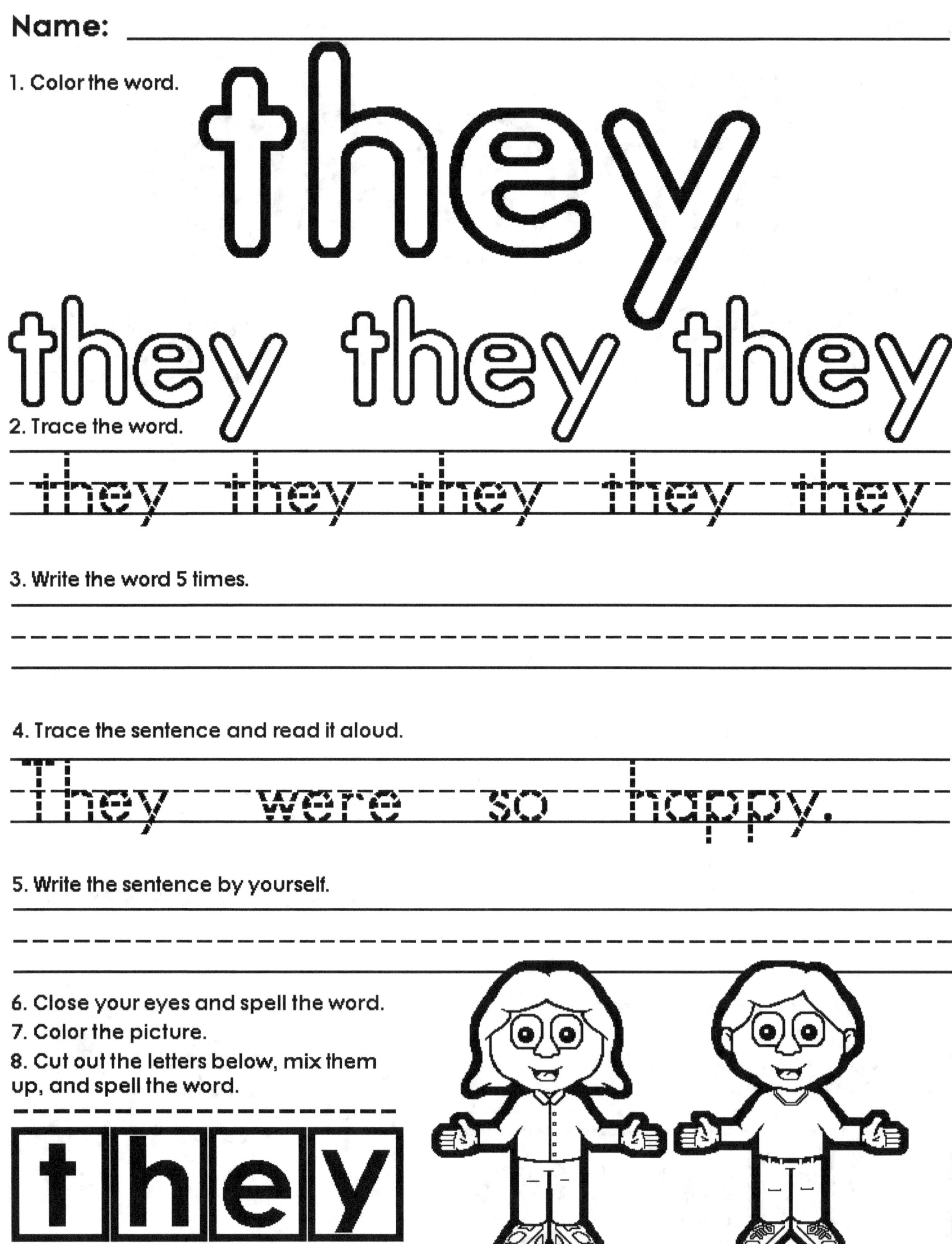

1. Color the word.

this
this   this   this

2. Trace the word.

this   this   this   this   this

3. Write the word 5 times.

4. Trace the sentence and read it aloud.

This   is   my   hammer.

5. Write the sentence by yourself.

6. Close your eyes and spell the word.

7. Color the picture.

8. Cut out the letters below, mix them up, and spell the word.

t h i s

Name: ___________________________________

1. Color the word.

time
time time time

2. Trace the word.

time   time   time   time   time

3. Write the word 5 times.

4. Trace the sentence and read it aloud.

It is time to go.

5. Write the sentence by yourself.

©2020 SightWordRainbow.com

6. Close your eyes and spell the word.
7. Color the picture.
8. Cut out the letters below, mix them up, and spell the word.

t i m e

Name: _______________________________

1. Color the word.

to   to   to   to   to

2. Trace the word.

to   to   to   to   to

3. Write the word 5 times.

4. Trace the sentence and read it aloud.

I like to hop.

5. Write the sentence by yourself.

6. Close your eyes and spell the word.
7. Color the picture.
8. Cut out the letters below, mix them up, and spell the word.

t o

Name: ______________________________

1. Color the word.

up

up up up up

2. Trace the word.

up up up up up

3. Write the word 5 times.

4. Trace the sentence and read it aloud.

The sun is up.

5. Write the sentence by yourself.

6. Close your eyes and spell the word.
7. Color the picture.
8. Cut out the letters below, mix them up, and spell the word.

U P

Name: _______________________________

1. Color the word.

use

use   use   use

2. Trace the word.

use   use   use   use   use

3. Write the word 5 times.

4. Trace the sentence and read it aloud.

I use a pencil.

5. Write the sentence by yourself.

6. Close your eyes and spell the word.
7. Color the picture.
8. Cut out the letters below, mix them up, and spell the word.

u s e

Name: ______________________

1. Color the word.

very

very very very

2. Trace the word.

very very very very very

3. Write the word 5 times.

4. Trace the sentence and read it aloud.

The monkey is very silly.

5. Write the sentence by yourself.

6. Close your eyes and spell the word.
7. Color the picture.
8. Cut out the letters below, mix them up, and spell the word.

v e r y

1. Color the word.

was

was was was

2. Trace the word.

was   was   was   was   was

3. Write the word 5 times.

4. Trace the sentence and read it aloud.

A dinosaur was very big.

5. Write the sentence by yourself.

6. Close your eyes and spell the word.
7. Color the picture.
8. Cut out the letters below, mix them up, and spell the word.

w a s

1. Color the word.

we

we   we   we

2. Trace the word.

we   we   we   we   we

3. Write the word 5 times.

4. Trace the sentence and read it aloud.

We   like   to   run.

5. Write the sentence by yourself.

©2020 SightWordRainbow.com

6. Close your eyes and spell the word.
7. Color the picture.
8. Cut out the letters below, mix them up, and spell the word.

Name: ___________________________

1. Color the word.

2. Trace the word.

were were were were were

3. Write the word 5 times.

4. Trace the sentence and read it aloud.

They were all on the log.

5. Write the sentence by yourself.

©2020 SightWordRainbow.com

6. Close your eyes and spell the word.

7. Color the picture.

8. Cut out the letters below, mix them up, and spell the word.

1. Color the word.

2. Trace the word.

3. Write the word 5 times.

4. Trace the sentence and read it aloud.

5. Write the sentence by yourself.

©2020 SightWordRainbow.com

6. Close your eyes and spell the word.
7. Color the picture.
8. Cut out the letters below, mix them up, and spell the word.

Name: ___________________________

1. Color the word.

when

when   when

2. Trace the word.

when when when when when

3. Write the word 5 times.

4. Trace the sentence and read it aloud.

When can we go?

5. Write the sentence by yourself.

©2020 SightWordRainbow.com

6. Close your eyes and spell the word.

7. Color the picture.

8. Cut out the letters below, mix them up, and spell the word.

1. Color the word.

where
where   where

2. Trace the word.

where where where where

3. Write the word 4 times.

4. Trace the sentence and read it aloud.

Where did the ship go?

5. Write the sentence by yourself.

©2020 SightWordRainbow.com

6. Close your eyes and spell the word.

7. Color the picture.

8. Cut out the letters below, mix them up, and spell the word.

1. Color the word.

which

which   which

2. Trace the word.

which   which   which   which

3. Write the word 4 times.

4. Trace the sentence and read it aloud.

Which animal is on top?

5. Write the sentence by yourself.

©2020 SightWordRainbow.com

6. Close your eyes and spell the word.

7. Color the picture.

8. Cut out the letters below, mix them up, and spell the word.

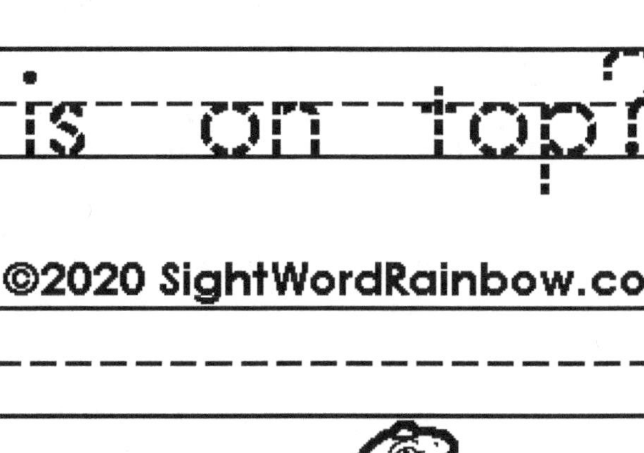

Name: _______________________

1. Color the word.

who

who who who

2. Trace the word.

who who who who who

3. Write the word 5 times.

4. Trace the sentence and read it aloud.

Who is she?

5. Write the sentence by yourself.

6. Close your eyes and spell the word.
7. Color the picture.
8. Cut out the letters below, mix them up, and spell the word.

w h o

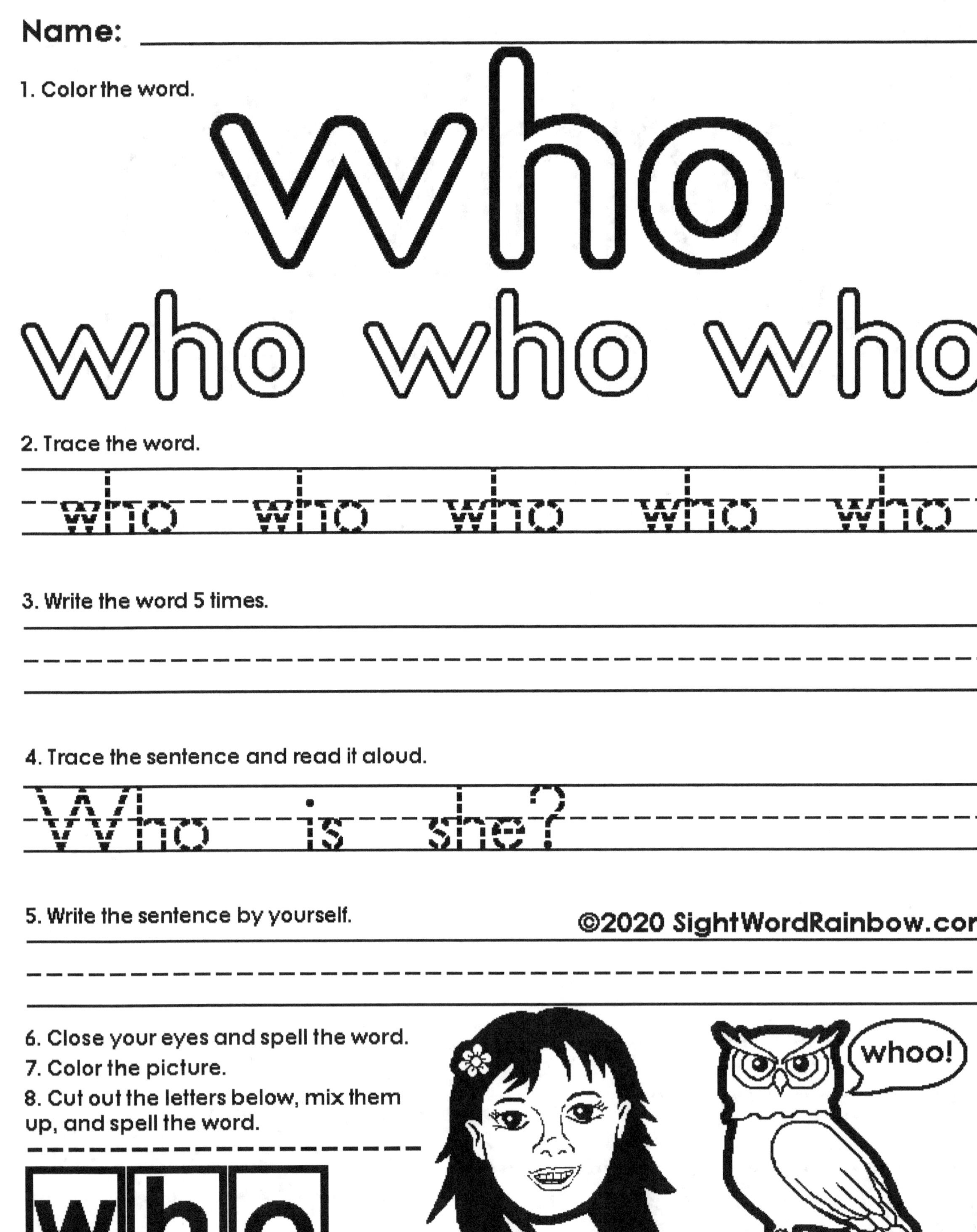

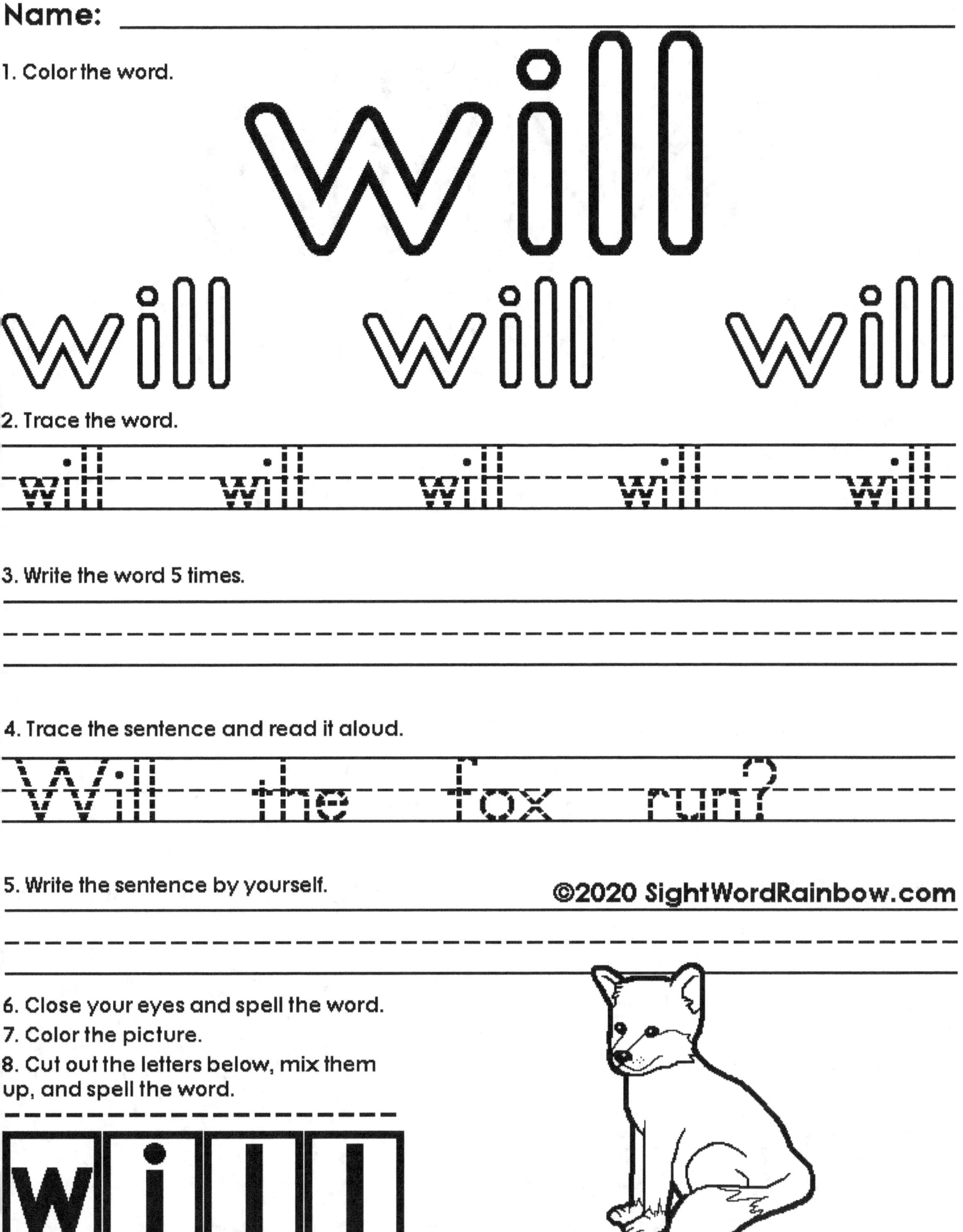

Name: _______________________________

1. Color the word.

will

will   will   will

2. Trace the word.

will   will   will   will   will

3. Write the word 5 times.

4. Trace the sentence and read it aloud.

Will the fox run?

5. Write the sentence by yourself.

©2020 SightWordRainbow.com

6. Close your eyes and spell the word.

7. Color the picture.

8. Cut out the letters below, mix them up, and spell the word.

w i l l

1. Color the word.

with
with with with

2. Trace the word.

with with with with with

3. Write the word 5 times.

4. Trace the sentence and read it aloud.

Can I go with you?

5. Write the sentence by yourself.

©2020 SightWordRainbow.com

6. Close your eyes and spell the word.
7. Color the picture.
8. Cut out the letters below, mix them up, and spell the word.

w i t h

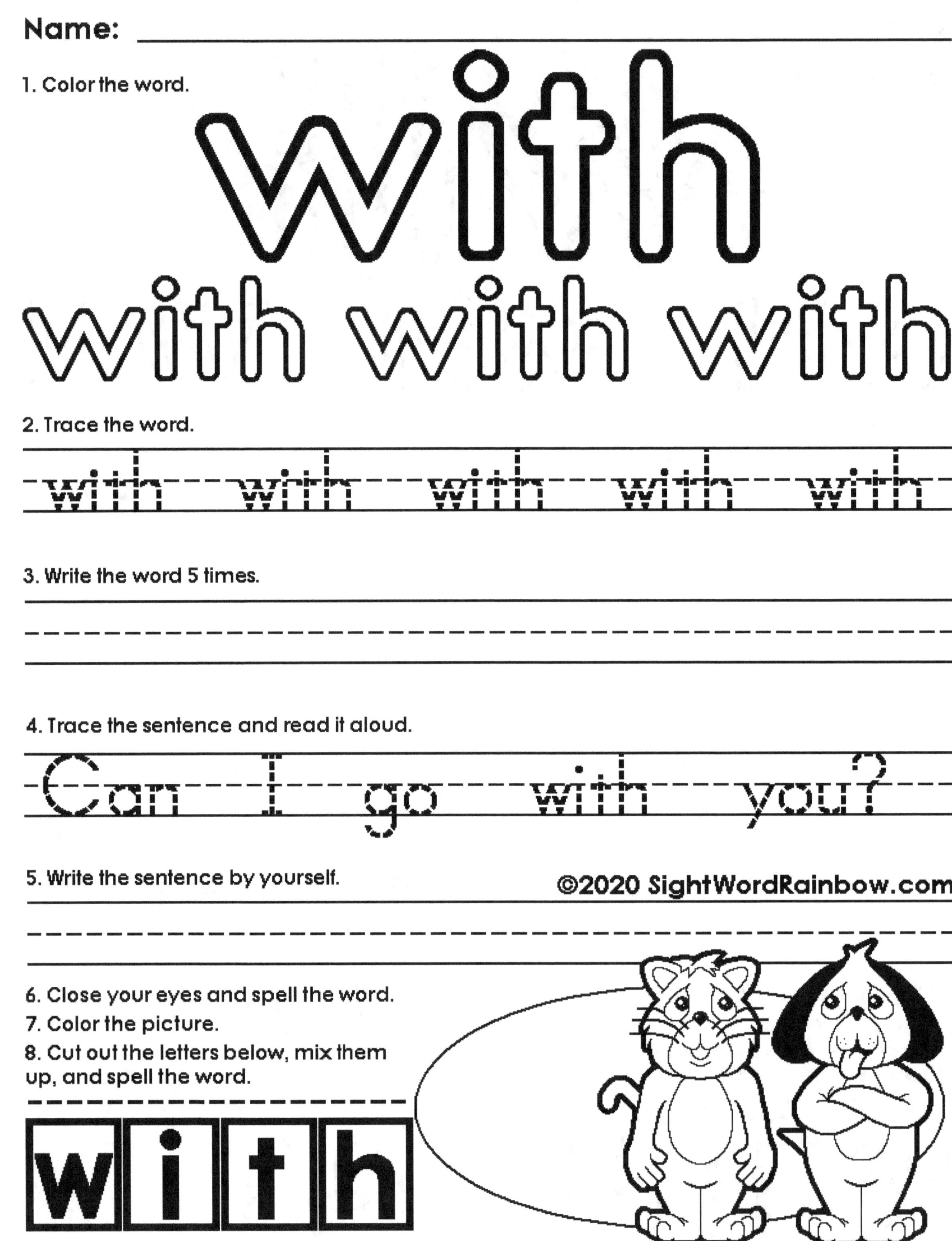

Name: ____________________

1. Color the word.

words
words   words

2. Trace the word.

words   words   words   words

3. Write the word 4 times.

4. Trace the sentence and read it aloud.

These words are very long!

5. Write the sentence by yourself.

©2020 SightWordRainbow.com

6. Close your eyes and spell the word.
7. Color the words.
8. Cut out the letters below, mix them up, and spell the word.

w o r d s

helicopter
pumpkin
bathroom

Name: _______________________________

1. Color the word.

would

would   would

2. Trace the word.

would   would   would   would

3. Write the word 4 times.

4. Trace the sentence and read it aloud.

Would you like some gum?

5. Write the sentence by yourself.

6. Close your eyes and spell the word.
7. Color the picture.
8. Cut out the letters below, mix them
up, and spell the word.

w o u l d

Name: _______________________

1. Color the word.

you

you   you   you

2. Trace the word.

you   you   you   you   you

3. Write the word 5 times.

4. Trace the sentence and read it aloud.

Can you see it?

5. Write the sentence by yourself.

©2020 SightWordRainbow.com

6. Close your eyes and spell the word.

7. Color the picture.

8. Cut out the letters below, mix them up, and spell the word.

y o u

Name: _______________________________

1. Color the word.

your

your your your

2. Trace the word.

your your your your your

3. Write the word 5 times.

4. Trace the sentence and read it aloud.

Is this your bear?

5. Write the sentence by yourself.

©2020 SightWordRainbow.com

6. Close your eyes and spell the word.
7. Color the picture.
8. Cut out the letters below, mix them up, and spell the word.

y o u r